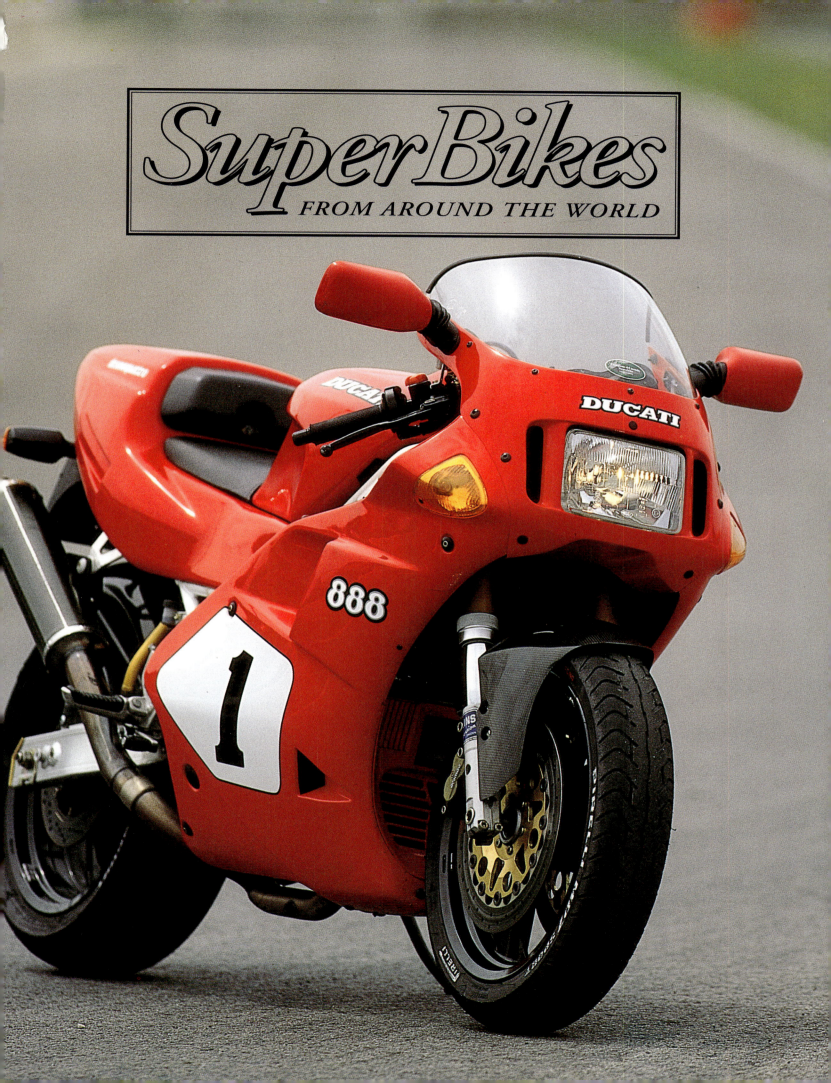

SuperBikes
FROM AROUND THE WORLD

SuperBikes

FROM AROUND THE WORLD

Edited by Mac McDiarmid
with contributions by
Tom Isitt and Kevin Raymond

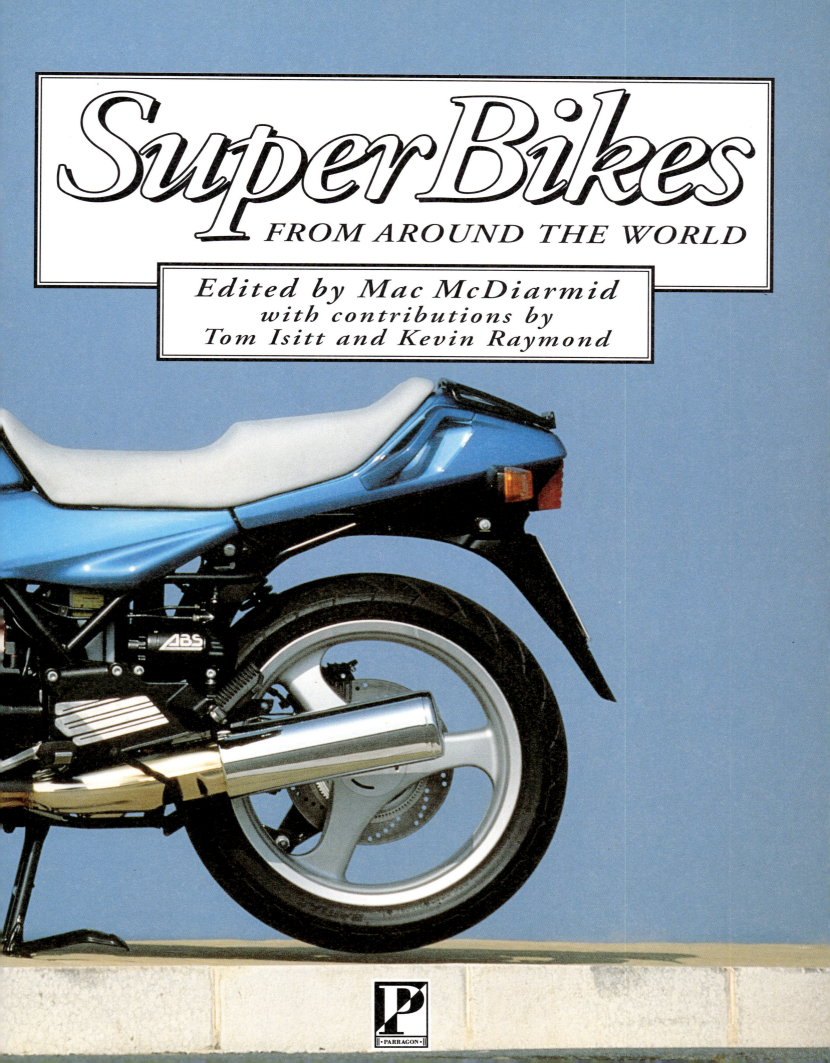

PARRAGON

Page 1 — A house-trained racer — but only just — the exquisite Ducati 888SPS is one of the rarest sights on the road.

Pages 2-3 — Fuel-injected K1100RS is the pinnacle of BMW's enduring pursuit of the perfect high-speed tourer.

First Published in Great Britain in 1996 by
Parragon Books Limited
Units 13-17, Avonbridge Industrial Estate
Atlantic Road, Avonmouth, Bristol BS11 9QD
United Kingdom

Designed and produced by
Stonecastle Graphics Limited
Old Chapel Studio, Plain Road, Marden
Tonbridge, Kent TN12 9LS United Kingdom

© Parragon Books Limited 1996

ISBN 0-7525-1432-6

Printed in Great Britain

Photography credits

Roland Brown: pages 2-3, 15 (top), 16, 17, 18, 36, 37 (top)
Jason Critchell: 90, 91 (top)
Gold & Goose: page 54
David Goldman: pages 10 (top), 11, 14, 15 (bottom), 20, 21, 78, 79 (bottom)
Patrick Gosling: 52, 53
Harley-Davidson: page 37 (bottom), 38
Honda UK: page 41
Mac McDiarmid: pages 1, 7, 10 (bottom), 22, 25 (right), 26, 28, 29, 34, 35, 42, 43, 44, 45, 48, 49, 51, 56, 57, 58, 64, 65, 69, 74, 75 (top), 77, 79 (top), 88 (top), 89, 92, 93, 94, 95
Phil Masters: pages 27 (bottom), 30, 31, 62, 63, 76, 82, 83
Mitsui Yamaha: page 84, 86, 88 (bottom)
Kenny P: pages 8, 9, 85, 87
Kevin Raymond: 50
Garry Stuart: pages 46, 47
Suzuki GB: 71 (bottom right)
Oli Tennent: pages 5, 6, 12, 13, 23, 24, 25, 27 (top), 32, 33, 39, 40, 19, 55, 58, 59, 60, 61, 66, 67, 70, 71 (top), 72, 73, 75 (bottom), 80, 81, 91 (bottom)
to all of whom, many thanks.

Contents

Harley-Davidson Heritage Softail — proving there's sometimes more to superbikes than super performance.

Introduction

....

'A Superbike, then, is something which stands out from the common herd of two-wheelers.'

Although the word 'Superbike' didn't exist before 1969, the concept certainly did. Coined to express the sense of wonder at Honda's then new CB750-four, it might equally have been used in an earlier age to describe a Brough Superior, a Vincent Black Shadow, or even the Triumph and BSA triples which preceded the Honda by a mere year.

In some ways it is a trite expression, no more worthy of our esteem than various 'superstars' or 'supermodels'. And there is, after all, nothing very exhilarating about a 'super' market. Yet 'superbike' is also shorthand for the bewildering technical advances of motorcycling over the past 30 years. In previous times, truly outstanding machines might appear perhaps once per decade; by the early 'seventies perhaps once per year; now they're coming at us thick and fast.

So exactly what does put the 'super' into 'Superbike'? Literally, the prefix means 'above'. It can mean, and it certainly does here, 'superior in quality . . . a degree beyond the ordinary meaning'. A Superbike, then, is something set apart from the common herd of two-wheelers. It is so special that the mere words 'bike', or 'motorcycle' cannot fully fully describe it. A Superbike stands out.

It does not simply mean 'faster'. Nor does it refer to price. The very fastest and most expensive motorcycles, certainly, are Superbikes. But so are some of the slowest – at least if you allow Harley-Davidson into the equation. In their case, the 'degree extra' is some indefinable quality. It isn't simply style and it certainly isn't performance, but most motorcyclists recognise it when they see it.

That, perhaps, is the essence of the true

Honda's CBR900RR Fireblade redefined the superbike concept when launched in 1992, and still reigns supreme amongst Japanese supersport fours.

Superbike. Whatever physical properties they may have, they also possess something extra, some indefinable quality which sets them apart. Inevitably, it is subjective and open to argument. And it is by no means always the same. Whatever it is about a Harley that turns people on, Bimotas have something very different but equally desirable.

Whatever that quality might be, all the motorcycles on the following pages have it – from the sensuous good looks of Ducati's 916 to the brutal elegance of Yamaha's XJR1200. From the over-the-top specification of Honda's GL1500 Gold Wing to the sheer bruising speed of Kawasaki's ZZ-R1100. From the stylised Retro-tech of Harley-Davidson's Heritage Softail, to the brave novelty of Bimota's Tesi 1D. From the breathtaking power-to-weight of the Honda CBR900RR Fireblade, to the understated efficiency of the BMW K1100RS.

Ironically, a common complaint about modern motorcycles is that they are 'all becoming the same'. Yet even a cursory inspection of these Superbikes reveals a mouth-watering diversity of form and function. Turn the pages, relish them, and dream. For these are not merely motorcycles, they are fantasies given physical form. 'Superbike' is really too humble a word to describe them.

Not quite the fastest, but perhaps the sexiest superbike ever built, Ducati's 916 is also almost unbeatable on the track.

Nico Bakker QCS1000

....

> *'The svelte bodywork and 'unusual' suspension systems give the QCS a look all its own.'*

Only a handful of exotic bikes have single-sided suspension at even one end. Only Nico Bakker's creation boasts such technology at both.

Yamaha were the first company to put an alternative front end into mass production on a motorcycle, but they were by no means the first to experiment with replacing the front forks in favour of a better design.

One of the pioneers of alternative front ends is Dutch 'specials' builder Nico Bakker, a man with several decades of chassis and suspension building to his credit and an impressive consultancy list that includes BMW and Laverda. And his QCS1000 (QCS stands for Quick Change System – both wheels can be changed in a very short space of time) is the latest incarnation of his own very effective design.

Traditional front forks are inherently flexible and can affect a motorcycle's steering geometry as they compress in corners. A method of separating the steering from the front suspension is generally considered to be the way forward for motorcycle design, and as yet only Yamaha and BMW have put alternative front suspension systems into production. But Nico Bakker has a system which he has been using since 1988 which is both clever and effective.

The QCS is a hand-built 'special' that uses a Yamaha FZR1000 engine for its motive power, around which is wrapped an aluminium-alloy square-section chassis onto which are bolted single-sided swingarms front and back. The front suspension system works in a very similar way to that of the Yamaha GTS1000 – the steering is handled via a spar running from the hub of the front wheel to the steering crown, while the suspension is actuated by the single-sided swingarm that bolts onto the front of the chassis. The benefits of this system can best be realised by a high-performance

sportsbike, which makes Yamaha's decision to fit it to a modest-performance sports-tourer surprising.

But the performance of the QCS is anything but modest. The derestricted FZR1000 engine oozes power and torque. The five-valves-per-cylinder in-line four makes 145bhp in the QCS and is capable of whisking it up to 165mph in very short order.

The rear suspension is also a single-sided swingarm affair, but without the necessity for steering the system, is used primarily for fast wheel changes (Honda developed this system for their endurance racing bikes, and it has subsequently been used on road-going machines by Honda and Aprilia).

On the road the QCS delivers exactly what it promises. There is no front end dive when hard on the brakes, and the bike is rock-steady mid-turn. It exhibits none of the drawbacks of traditional front forks and, unlike the GTS1000, the steering response is both fast and positive. A massive front

disc brake gripped by a six-piston caliper helps stop this 160mph beast, and a massive 180/55 section rear tyre helps the QCS grip tenaciously in the corners.

The svelte bodywork and 'unusual' suspension systems give the QCS a look all of its own – the swoopy styling and bright red paint tells the world that this is one serious, and very purposeful, motorcycle.

Very much more than a mere styling exercise, the QCS combines stability and agility in unprecedented proportions.

SPECIFICATION: NICO BAKKER QCS1000	
ENGINE	Water-cooled DOHC 20-valve in-line four
DISPLACEMENT	1002cc
HORSEPOWER	145bhp @ 10,000rpm
CARBURETTORS	4 x 38mm Mikuni
GEAR BOX	Six speed
FRAME	Aluminium-alloy twin beam
WHEELBASE	57ins
WEIGHT	418lbs dry
TOP SPEED	165mph

Bimota Furano

The hand-crafted light alloy beam frame is a Rimini hallmark, along with exquisite attention to detail and — usually above all — ferocious performance.

P owerful, light and stunningly fast, Bimota's Furano was arguably the finest sports bike in the world when it was launched in 1992 — as well as one of the most expensive.

The Furano, named after a wind that blew across the Adriatic sea near Bimota's base in Rimini, combined a tuned version of the 1002cc four-cylinder engine from Yamaha's FZR1000 with a light and exotic chassis of the Italian firm's own design. The bike was hand-built in numbers of just 100 to provide the ultimate in high-speed motorcycling.

The FZR was a fine sports machine in its own right, so using its engine was an excellent starting point. In standard form the twin-cam, 20-valve lump produced 140bhp with generous midrange torque. Bimota added a Weber-Marelli fuel-injection set-up and replaced the four-into-one exhaust system with a lighter, less-restrictive design of their own. The result was a claimed peak output of 164bhp at 10,500rpm.

The engine was bolted to a typical Bimota frame consisting of two aviation-alloy spars, each one hugely thick, beautifully machined and immensely strong. Suspension parts came from Swedish firm Öhlins, widely regarded as the best in the world. Both the upside-down front forks and single rear shock absorber were fully adjustable for both compression and rebound damping.

Other cycle-parts were of equally high specification. The front brake comprised two 320mm diameter drilled Brembo discs, gripped by four-piston calipers. Wheels were composite, 17-inch diameter items of Bimota's own design; tyres were soft-compound Michelin radials, the massive rear cover measuring over seven inches in width.

Bimota's traditionally high quality of finish was particularly evident in the bodywork, in which reinforcing patches of lightweight carbon-fibre were visible amid the hand-painted fibreglass of the one-piece fairing and seat-tank unit. (Bimota claimed the fibre-bonding

Keeping up with — and usually ahead of — the mass-produced motorcycling Jones's is ever the Bimota goal.

process was so complex that one fairing in three was rejected.) More carbon-fibre was used for parts such as mudguards and silencer.

The result was a dry weight of 396lb – typical of a 600cc middleweight rather than a full-blown superbike – which gave the Furano an unrivalled power to weight ratio. Combined with the fuel-injection's crisp response, the result was awesome acceleration. At about 4000rpm in first gear, a flick of the wrist sent the front wheel hurtling skywards as the Furano stormed forward with its tacho needle sweeping towards the 11,500rpm redline.

Few roadgoing vehicles could come even close to matching the Furano, which flashed from 0-60mph in the flicker of a stopwatch, and screamed through the standing quarter-mile in under 11 seconds. Top speed was predictably mind-blowing, too, with more than 170mph available given the right gearing and a clear stretch of tarmac.

Even more impressive was the Bimota's handling, particularly the ultra-responsive feel derived from the blend of rigid frame, taut suspension and premium rubber. The Furano gave no hint of a wobble even at the highest speeds. Steering was quick and precise; the bike could be slowed hard with a brush of the

potent Brembos, flicked into corners with a minimum of effort, then powered out with the fat rear tyre welded to the road.

Advances in Japanese sports bike design meant the Furano could not hope to match the edge that some of its Bimota predecessors had enjoyed over the competition. Mass-produced Japanese rivals such as Honda's CBR900RR, in particular, provided high power outputs and excellent handling. The Bimota justified its far higher price by being not only even faster and more agile but also much rarer and more exotic. It was a hand-built, lavishly equipped superbike created simply to be the fastest and best in the world.

Few bikes — and none with comparable performance — hurtle into bends with quite the controlled flair of the Furano.

SPECIFICATION: BIMOTA FURANO	
ENGINE	Water-cooled DOHC 20-valve in-line four
DISPLACEMENT	1002cc
HORSEPOWER	164bhp @ 10,500rpm
CARBURETTORS	Weber fuel-injection
GEAR BOX	Five speed
FRAME	Aluminium alloy twin beam
WHEELBASE	55.9ins
WEIGHT	396lbs dry
TOP SPEED	172mph

'Few roadgoing vehicles could come even close to matching the Furano.'

Bimota SB6

'The SB6 steers and handles like a well set-up race bike.'

Audacious SB6 styling was a new departure for Bimota. Delicious execution, outrageous performance and sheer desirability were not.

Bimota's reputation for providing the ultimate in motorcycling thrills had come under threat during the early 'nineties. Honda's Fireblade, in particular, had proved the Japanese could build light, powerful machines that were anything but bland. Bimota's Yamaha-engined YB8 series was still going strong, but the styling was starting to look a little dated next to the Fireblade and, especially, Ducati's landmark 916.

The search for an engine to power a new flagship sports bike ended when Suzuki introduced the water-cooled GSX-R1100. In full power form, and with a less restrictive exhaust and intake, the Suzuki engine was capable of over 155bhp – 30bhp more than even the best standard Fireblade. Married to an all-new, amazingly compact aluminium chassis, it made for a formidable combination of light weight (just slightly more than the Fireblade) and razor-sharp handling.

At first glance, the SB6 looks like a 600, or a 750 at most – it's that small. With a microscopic wheelbase of just 54.2in, it steers like a 600 too, and you can put total confidence in the wide front tyre's ability to cope with fast direction changes.

But it's when you open the throttle that the SB6 really shows its true colours. This is possibly the most violently explosive acceleration you'll find on any road bike. It will quite happily wheelie over backwards in second gear if the rider isn't concentrating, and will rocket on to well over 170mph in the right conditions.

That's OK in a straight line, but putting that sort of power onto the road coming out of corners needs top-notch suspension and chassis components, and wide, sticky tyres.

It will come as no surprise to anyone who's ever recoiled in shock at a Bimota price list that the SB6 has the lot. The aluminium chassis is massively stiff, and combines with 46mm Paoli front forks and an Öhlins rear suspension unit to provide superb control both through bends and as the Bim's immense power is applied. Completing the handling package, ultra-light magnesium alloy wheels wear semi-race compound Michelin Tyres.

Braking, too, is handled by some of the best equipment on the market. Brembo 320mm fully floating front discs are gripped by race-spec calipers capable of locking the front wheel at 170mph.

SPECIFICATION: BIMOTA SB6	
ENGINE	Water-cooled DOHC
	16-valve in-line four
DISPLACEMENT	1074cc
HORSEPOWER	156bhp @ 10,000
CARBURETTORS	4 x 40mm Mikuni
GEAR BOX	Five speed
FRAME	Aluminium twin spar
WHEELBASE	54.2ins
WEIGHT	419lbs dry
TOP SPEED	175mph

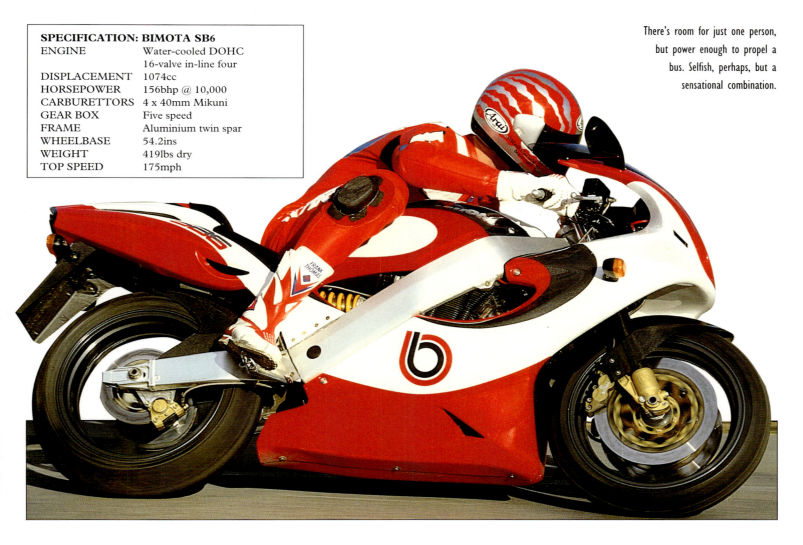

There's room for just one person, but power enough to propel a bus. Selfish, perhaps, but a sensational combination.

The equipment list may be impressive, but even more so is the way all the individual components are balanced and harmonised to produce a bike that is far more than a pretty spec sheet. The SB6 steers and handles like a well set-up race bike, and there are very few riders – and even fewer public roads – capable of doing it justice. Those who wish to try will need to be sufficiently well-heeled; Bimota ownership never did come cheap, and the SB6 is nearly twice the price of the Suzuki from which it takes its engine.

But the price starts to look less important the closer you look at what you get for your money. Impressive as the SB6 is on the move, there's just as much enjoyment to be had simply taking in all the exquisite details of milled and turned alloy that Bimota, as a tiny volume producer, can justify where the big factories use plain, heavy castings. The swoopy, heavily styled carbon fibre bodywork is finished in paint with gloss a mile deep, and the carbon fibre touches extend to the front and rear mudguards.

There's no space for a pillion. No one in their right mind would want to upset the equilibrium of such a finely balanced creation – it would be like a asking a Derby winner to pull a milk cart.

If you want practicality, look elsewhere. The SB6 exists for one reason only: to put the most power in the smallest space, under the best control.

Huge Paoli forks, Öhlins rear suspension, Brembo discs and sticky Michelin tyres do everything technically possible to keep the SB6 under control. The rest is up to the rider.

Bimota Tesi 1D

....

'The whole bike is clad in carbon-fibre bodywork and equipped with a pair of Kevlar silencers.'

The Bimota Tesi is one of the most radical, extraordinary and most interesting superbikes ever built. With the Tesi, the small Italian factory took a giant leap forward in motorcycle design, one that only Yamaha (and to a lesser extent BMW) have dared to follow, although 'specials' builders such as Nico Bakker have produced similar machines in very small numbers. What Bimota did was put into production a superbike that featured hub-centre steering rather than traditional telescopic front forks.

The problem with conventional telescopic forks is that they flex under braking and cornering, and because they compress under braking, the steering geometry of the bike is altered. In an ideal world the suspension and steering of a motorcycle should be separate and independent to each other. With telescopic forks this isn't possible, no matter how good the forks are, but with hub-centre steering the suspension can be separated from the steering.

So instead of wrapping the motorcycle's engine in a conventional frame and then bolting a pair of forks to the headstock and a rear swingarm to the back, Bimota have wrapped their chassis around the sides of the engine and then bolted a swingarm on at the front and at the back. The rear swingarm pivots in the traditional way and actuates the rear shock, while the front shock is bolted to the left-hand spar of the front swingarm and to the chassis. A complicated system of linkages joins the steering column to the front wheel to allow almost 30 degrees of steering movement.

One of the advantages of using a twin-sided front swingarm (as opposed to a single-sided one like the Yamaha GTS1000) is that it allows two brake discs to be used. And with twin 320mm front discs gripped by four-piston Brembo calipers, the Tesi has one of the best brake set-ups of any superbike.

All Bimotas are beautiful. The Tesi adds technical novelty to the usual aesthetic flair of Rimini products.

'Tesi' is Italian for degree thesis — of Bimota designer Pierluigi Marconi. If only all university courses looked like this.

The engine itself is a modified version of the Ducati 904cc water-cooled eight-valve desmodromic V-twin engine which uses a development of the Weber-Marelli fuel-injection system to produce a hefty 117bhp.

If all this doesn't sound exotic enough, the whole bike is clad in carbon-fibre bodywork and equipped with a pair of Kevlar silencers. The finished result is a bike that scales a featherweight 407lbs dry and which has a wheelbase more akin to a 400cc machine than a litre bike.

On the road the Tesi is quite unlike anything else. The lack of dive when slowing, and the fact that the suspension continues to work during hard braking, means that the Tesi can be braked later and cornered harder than anything else on the road. The fire-breathing Ducati engine means that top speeds of 160mph are a breeze and that in terms of performance the Tesi will stay with the very best that Japan has to offer.

The down side is that the Tesi is a solo machine, with no accommodation for pillion passengers, and it costs twice as much as a Yamaha GTS1000. In fact, except for the Honda NR750, the Tesi is the most expensive production bike in the world. But then it is also arguably the best production bike in the world.

Unique Tesi front suspension comes into its own, howling into bumpy corners hard on the brakes.

SPECIFICATION: BIMOTA TESI 1D	
ENGINE	Water-cooled SOHC 8-valve Desmo V-twin
DISPLACEMENT	904cc
HORSEPOWER	117bhp
CARBURETTORS	Electronic fuel injection
GEAR BOX	6 speed
FRAME	Twin aluminium-alloy plates
WHEELBASE	55.5ins
WEIGHT	407lbs dry
TOP SPEED	160mph

BMW K1100RS

'High-speed stability is excellent, as befits a long-haul sports tourer.'

Although reminiscent of the K100RS of ten years earlier, the 1100 has evolved into something far more flexible and assured.

BMW are not slavish followers of fashion. The Bavarian company resolutely goes its own way, largely ignoring the trends elsewhere yet sustaining a peerless reputation for excellence.

For decades the BMW way was based around a single engine format, the horizontally-opposed 'Boxer' twin evolved from Max Friz' original design of 1923. But 12 years ago, in the face of growing performance expectations fuelled by Japanese and Italian Superbikes, they produced their first modern multi. Although a four, like so many others, it was again uniquely BMW. For not only did the engine sit fore-and-aft in the frame, but it also lay on its side. It was immediately christened the 'Flying Brick'. BMW are nothing if not different.

From the original 1000cc 8-valve K100 of 1983 evolved a 750cc triple, the K75. Both engines were produced in various model guises – basic unfaired, touring and sports-touring. The latter, designated 'RS', was the flagship of the range. In 1989, a 16-valve cylinder head was introduced, initially for the surpassingly ugly K1, but later for other top-of-the-range models. For 1992, an 1100cc (actually 1092cc) version was developed for the K1100RT tourer, producing the same 100bhp as before but with a generous helping of extra mid-range torque. A year later the big engine was grafted into the sports tourer: the K1100RS.

Taking out capacity from 987 to 1092cc makes the 1100 one of the all-time torque kings. Peak

torque rose from 74lb.ft at a fairly giddy (for BMW) 6750rpm to 79lb.ft at a comparatively sedate 5500. More telling still is the sheer spread of torque: at a mere 2000rpm, the engine is three-quarters as grunty as it ever gets.

Putting this to the road is the familiar BMW five speed gearbox, via the even more traditional dry, single plate clutch and shaft final drive. But, for a marque once maligned for its gearchange, the latest BMWs are as positive and slick as big bikes come.

This doesn't translate – quite – into neck-snapping getaways. At 550lb, the RS is too heavy for that. But, allied to supremely well-metered electronic fuel injection, it does translate into a relentless responsiveness that few other machines can match.

The suspension, whilst still fairly softly-sprung, is far better controlled than on BMWs of a decade ago. At the rear is the unique Paralever system first introduced on the GS twin. Using a Japanese Showa shock, its geometry is complex, but is an attempt both to increase stability and reduce the inbuilt tendency of shaft drive to compromise the action of the rear suspension. On both counts, it works well.

The front suspension is less radical than the Telelever fitted elsewhere in the BMW range. Superficially, it uses 42mm telescopic forks similar to those on the 100RS of ten years ago. That was a vague, wallowy device, but the 1100's action is altogether firmer and better damped. High-speed stability is excellent, as befits a long-haul sports tourer. Nonetheless this is a heavy, tall and rather cumbersome motorcycle better suited to autobahns than back roads.

BMWs are often described as more than the sum of their parts, and the K1100RS is no exception. The riding position and seat come together to provide one of the kindest, most relaxed perches in motorcycling, whilst the excellent fairing minimises rider fatigue. The Brembo brakes, with ABS standard in the UK, are superb. Add the usual BMW build quality, classy, timeless looks, an extensive range of luggage and accessories, and the K1100RS comes together as the grand tourer supreme.

Race replica handling has never been a BMW priority, so much as long-haul comfort and a compliant ride.

SPECIFICATION: BMW K1100RS	
ENGINE	Liquid-cooled DOHC 16-valve longitudinal four
DISPLACEMENT	1092cc
HORSEPOWER	100bhp @ 7500rpm
CARBURETTORS	Motronic electronic fuel injection
GEAR BOX	Five speed
FRAME	Tubular steel space frame
WHEELBASE	61.6ins
WEIGHT	547lbs
TOP SPEED	137mph

BMW R1100RS

·······························

'BMW designed this bike to be a superlative sport-tourer.'

BMW have a reputation for building top-quality touring motorcycles rather than high-performance superbikes, but in recent years they have managed to bridge the gap between the two concepts. Arguably the most eye-catching of this new breed is the R1100RS.

The R1100RS is a unique departure for BMW. Since the 1930s they have been building horizontally-opposed twin-cylinder machines with two valves per cylinder actuated by push-rods. But with the R1100RS the 'Boxer' engine (as it is commonly known) has joined the latter half of the 20th Century. It is still air cooled, but the number of valves per cylinder has been doubled to four, and their camshafts are now actuated by a series of belts driven from the crankshaft.

The old Bing carburettors, always a distinctive feature of the two-valve Boxer, have also been replaced – the R1100RS is the first Boxer to feature electronic fuel-injection.

But if all that is a major departure, the innovative 'Telelever' front suspension system of the R1100RS is a quantum leap into the next century for the German marque. Just as Yamaha has looked at alternative front suspension and steering systems for motorcycles, BMW has also taken the brave step of introducing their own solution to the problem. And that problem is that ideally the steering and suspension systems for a

motorcycle's front end should be separate and independent from each other. Traditional telescopic forks flex, the steering geometry of the machine is altered when the front brake is being used, and often much of the fork's movement is taken up with braking, leaving little to deal with bumps in the road.

Yamaha's solution to the problem is the hub-centre-steered GTS1000, but BMW have taken a lower-key approach. They still use a pair of telescopic forks on the R1100RS, but they deal with the steering only. The suspension is handled by a single shock absorber bolted to the headstock and actuated by a wishbone-shaped bracket that joins the forks to the chassis. In effect the forks are merely sliders that join the front wheel to the headstock, while the wishbone actuates the shock absorber. Thus the suspension and steering are separated, creating an anti-dive effect when the front brake is applied.

This system is much simpler than that used by the Yamaha GTS1000, but is no less effective. Indeed the consensus of opinion is that the BMW

This odd-looking thing is Bavaria's answer to riders who want '90s technology in a bike they can understand.

As well as scratching well (above), the *Bee-eM* offers more user-friendly 'goodies' than practically any other motorcycle.

Boxer engine is inevitably wide (left) but the RS still has plenty of ground clearance to exploit.

Telelever system is actually more effective than that of the Yamaha. Certainly the R1100RS gives more feedback to the rider, and retains the traditional look of telescopic forks – an important consideration for the normally conservative BMW buyer.

But there's more to the R1100RS than an all-new Boxer engine and a 'funny' front end. BMW designed this bike to be a superlative sport-tourer, so comfort and the ability to cover ground effortlessly are also essential. To this end BMW have equipped the R1100RS with a host of user-friendly features that include adjustable seat height, handlebars and windscreen to enable the owner to tailor the bike to his own requirements. Hard luggage as an optional extra which, allied to a five-gallon fuel tank and a frugal 45mpg fuel consumption, means the R1100RS can cover well over 200 miles to a tankful of fuel and pack a decent amount of luggage for the two-wheeled tourist.

Weighing in at 526lb, the BMW needs good brakes, so the R1100RS has a pair of 305mm discs at the front gripped by four-piston calipers. BMW's excellent anti-lock braking system is also fitted, making this a very safe and well-braked machine. With the engine putting out 95bhp the R1100RS is capable of topping 135mph, but it is its ability to cruise all day at three-figure speeds that is its forte.

What BMW have done is build a thoroughly modern motorcycle that should appeal to the traditionalist buyer in search of something a little different. It's not the fastest machine on the roads, but it is supremely capable, and – the Bavarian hallmark – resolutely unorthodox.

SPECIFICATION: BMW R1100RS SE	
ENGINE	Air-cooled horizontally-opposed eight-valve flat twin.
DISPLACEMENT	1185cc
HORSEPOWER	95bhp @ 7250rpm
CARBURETTORS	Electronic fuel injection
GEAR BOX	Five speed
FRAME	Tubular steel
WHEELBASE	58ins
WEIGHT	526lbs wet
TOP SPEED	135mph

Buell RS 1200

·························

*H*arley-Davidson's traditional concentration on cruisers and tourers has, over the years, led many smaller firms to produce sports bikes powered by the Milwaukee company's trademark V-twin engine. Most successful has been Erik Buell, a former road-racer and Harley engineer, whose series of innovative bikes have justified Buell's slogan: 'America's Faaast Motorcycle'.

Buell's first model, the RR1000, combined a tuned V-twin powerplant and lightweight chassis with aerodynamic, all-enveloping bodywork that boosted straight-line speed. The RR was successful in twin-cylinder racing, and made a swift and singleminded road bike too. Trouble was, nobody could tell its engine was a Harley unit – so in 1989 Buell produced a new model called the RS1200.

The RS featured broadly similar engineering to the RR, but the fully-enclosed bodywork was gone. Instead there was a sleekly integrated half-fairing, which put on display not only the all-important 1200 Sportster powerplant, but also the ingenious chassis that had also previously been buried behind fibreglass.

Buell's 'Uniplanar' frame design combined a Ducati-style ladder of slender steel tubes with a unique anti-vibration system. Four adjustable rods, each joining engine and frame, restricted the 45-degree V-twin motor's shaking to the vertical plane only. The design added engine stiffness to the chassis without passing vibration to the rider.

Other chassis details were equally clever, notably the RS1200's Marzocchi forks, which were fitted with Buell's own anti-dive system. The Works Performance rear shock unit was placed horizontally beneath the engine, and was adapted to extend over bumps – the opposite of a normal shock action.

Brakes and wheels were also of Buell's own design. The 17-inch wheels were made from polished aluminium, and held broad, sticky Dunlop Elite tyres. Big twin front discs were gripped by four-piston calipers, designed by Buell and built by specialists Performance Machine.

Too big to hide, too brutal to ignore, the tuned Harley engine sits proudly in Erik Buell's striking trellis frame.

A Harley that handles? Amazingly,
yes – if it's a Buell.

All bodywork was also shaped and created by Buell and his small team from Mukwanago, near Milwaukee in Wisconsin. The new fairing blended neatly into the tank/seat unit, while the seat featured a hump that hinged to become a pillion back-rest.

The Harley motor was left internally standard, and was boosted by a SuperTrapp exhaust system that raised its maximum output to about 60bhp at 5000rpm. Typically generous levels of low- and mid-range torque gave effortless acceleration with a twist of the throttle – and the Uniplanar system did a great job of controlling the V-twin's normal vibration. Even when revved hard, the Buell remained pleasantly smooth to a top speed of 120mph.

Equally importantly, the Buell's compact and well-appointed chassis meant that this was one Harley-engined bike that positively encouraged hard riding on twisty roads. The RS1200's racy steering geometry, excellent frame design and taut forks gave quick steering and flawless high-speed stability, though cornering was compromised slightly by the rather imprecise rear suspension set-up.

Buell's low production levels and labour-intensive assembly kept the RS1200's price high, but for riders who wanted a sporty Harley it was hard to beat. And that position changed in January 1993, when Harley-Davidson, keen to enter the sports bike market officially, bought a 49 per cent stake in Buell's company and raised the levels of investment, production and marketing.

In 1994 the renamed Buell Motorcycle Company launched its first bike, the S2 Thunderbolt – heavily based on the RS1200 but with numerous refinements in styling, power delivery and suspension. The Thunderbolt was a fast, fine-handling and handsome sports bike that was priced more competitively than ever. Boosted by Harley's backing, Buell looked set for an exciting future.

SPECIFICATION: BUELL RS1200	
ENGINE	Air-cooled pushrod OHV 45-degree V-twin
DISPLACEMENT	1200cc
HORSEPOWER	60bhp @ 5000rpm
CARBURETTORS	40mm Keihin
GEAR BOX	Four speed
FRAME	Tubular steel ladder
WHEELBASE	55.5ins
WEIGHT	450lbs dry
TOP SPEED	120mph

'Even when revved hard, the Buell remained pleasantly smooth to a top speed of 120mph.'

Cagiva 900 Elefant

....

'As a road bike the Elefant is surprisingly capable.'

Although based on Cagiva's successful desert racers, the Elefant is surprisingly adept at back-road scratching.

The popularity of the Paris-Dakar Rally in Europe has spawned a whole generation of enormous on/off-road superbikes, and none of them is more impressive than the Cagiva 900 Elefant.

The Paris-Dakar covered thousands of miles of desert in northern Africa, and the major motorcycle manufacturers spent many years, and enormous quantities of money, building bikes that would win it. Success in the Paris-Dakar translated directly to sales in Europe.

But the demands of the Saharan marathon meant that these trailbikes had to be very big and very fast, not something normally associated with off-road bikes. They also had to be immensely rugged and capable of carrying a lot of fuel and water with them – the two-wheeled equivalent of a Landcruiser.

The Cagiva 900 Elefant is a production version of the bike which triumphed in the Paris-Dakar a few years back, and is one of the biggest and best

Paris-Dakar replicas available. It's also one of the most interesting in that it uses a 900cc air and oil-cooled overhead cam 90-degree V-twin motor with desmodromic valve gear (as used on countless Ducati road and race bikes). Electronic fuel-injection helps the Elefant to produce a healthy 70bhp at 8500rpm, although brute power is less important with this kind of off-road machine than a usable spread of torque.

A high level of suspension equipment is *de rigeur* for desert-racers, and here the Cagiva gets full marks for Marzocchi forks at the front and an Öhlins multi-adjustable monoshock at the back. Rugged long-travel suspension is a must for this type of machine, and the Elefant has it in abundance.

Hefty twin front disc brakes give the Elefant plenty of stopping power, with twin-pot Nissin calipers providing bite. A large-capacity fuel tank (although not as large as the pukka desert race

bike's) and twin-headlamp fairing are also part of the essential P-D package, as is a vertiginous seat height of over 35ins.

As a road bike the Elefant is surprisingly capable. Although lacking the kind of power to compete directly with road-going sports 900s, the Elefant has a wide spread of power and torque which makes it very usable on twisting back roads. And with a top speed of 120mph the Elefant offers plenty of thrills along the way.

But it is off-road where the Cagiva really excels. That lazy, low-revving motor and low gearing make the Elefant a superb dirt bike that is equally at home idling along narrow gravel tracks or blasting at speed across open desert. The flexibility of the V-twin engine means that gear-changes are kept to a minimum, allowing the rider to concentrate on picking the right line across whatever terrain he happens to be traversing.

The long-travel suspension soaks up all but the biggest bumps, giving a soft manageable ride under almost all road and off-road conditions. That suspension travel also makes the Elefant a comfortable long-distance road mount, too.

Although bikes like the Elefant can't offer the kind of searing performance a high-performance road-bike can, their go-anywhere, do-anything capabilities give them an appeal all their own. The Cagiva 900 is undoubtedly the pinnacle of on/off-road engineering.

Gutsy V-twin power makes stunts such as this almost second nature. But if you want wild revs, look elsewhere.

Despite bash-plate and off-road styling, 900 Elefant is more a go-anywhere tourer than a true dirt machine.

SPECIFICATION: CAGIVA 900 ELEFANT	
ENGINE	Air/oil-cooled SOHC 90-degree Desmo V-twin
DISPLACEMENT	904cc
HORSEPOWER	70bhp @ 8500rpm
CARBURETTORS	Electronic fuel-injection
GEAR BOX	Five speed
FRAME	Aluminium-alloy cradle frame
WHEELBASE	61.8ins
WEIGHT	414lbs dry
TOP SPEED	120mph

Ducati 900 Monster

'All the elements come together to make a bike that is a real pleasure to ride, and even more of a pleasure to look at.'

Ducati made their reputation by building uncompromising sports bikes for those with the discernment and money to appreciate them, but in recent years they have branched out in another direction. In late '92 Ducati unveiled the M900 Monster to a stunned public, proving that they could build exciting bikes for all tastes, not just for the race replica sports rider.

The M900 was the first Ducati for many years to appeal to a wide range of riders, from the traditional Ducati fan to the rider in search of something 'a little different'. And the Monster is certainly different. Although it uses the same engine as the Ducati 900SS, the Monster is designed to be a muscle-bike. A bike that accelerates with startling rapidity, and which is more at home cruising the urban jungle looking for traffic-light Grands Prix to take part in than jockeying for position into turn one at Monza.

The Ducati 900SS has an engine blessed with masses of low-down power and usable torque, so to make it into a serious muscle-bike Ducati lowered the gearing and slotted the engine into the steel trellis frame that is their trademark. The engine puts out 84bhp at 7000rpm, power enough to hustle the Monster to a top speed of almost 130mph. That's not all that fast for a 900cc machine, but this is a bike built for cruising and back-road riding, so there is no fairing and the riding position is very upright. That makes it great in town or on country lanes, but painful at speed on motorways.

Where the Monster is really at home is cruising the *Promenade des Anglais* in Nice or parked outside *Tre Scalini* in the *Piazza Navonna* in Rome. This is a bike for being seen on, for posing on, for getting you around town in style and comfort, and with a large grin on your face.

And that grin is there not only because the Monster is very fast from a standing-start, not only because it is equipped with the best suspension and brakes around, but because it is a stupendous-looking machine. The feel-good factor gained from riding *Il Mostro* is enormous. Of course it does help that the Monster will out-drag all but the most powerful sports bike or supercar, that it comes with state-of-the-art 41mm upside-down forks and a multi-adjustable rear monoshock, and that it wears a massive pair of Brembo disc brakes equipped with four-piston calipers. All the elements come together to make a bike that is a real pleasure to ride, and even more of a pleasure to look at.

For the hard-core Ducati fan (a devotee of rock-solid suspension, agonising riding position, and 'idiosyncratic' electrics) the Monster will be a disappointment. But to everyone else the combination of good looks, lightning-quick steering, excellent suspension, eyeball-popping brakes and a lusty motor will ensure a huge grin and a much-depleted bank balance.

SPECIFICATION: DUCATI M900 MONSTER	
ENGINE	Air/oil-cooled SOHC 90-degree Desmo V-twin
DISPLACEMENT	904cc
HORSEPOWER	84bhp @ 7000rpm
CARBURETTORS	2 x 38mm Mikuni
GEAR BOX	Six speed
FRAME	Steel trellis
WHEELBASE	56.3ins
WEIGHT	408lbs
TOP SPEED	130mph

A rare picture of a M900 with both wheels on the ground. 'Wheelies' and 'stoppies' are more its natural territory.

Monster frame (above) comes from the 888 superbike, air-cooled engine from the familiar 900SS.

'Il Mostro' — the Monster — someone dubbed the prototype. Not surprisingly, the name stuck.

Ducati 888SPS

....

'Ride abruptly, and the head can wag in protest.'

To look at, this is just a Ducati SP4 with carbon-fibre silencer cans, a mere 25 million lira-worth. But it is more, much more than that. For what actually lurks beneath the scarlet bodywork is a slightly house-trained racing 'Corsa' engine, almost like Doug Polen's Superbike World championship winner. This is a Duke like no other. It's a Duke that power-wheelies in third, rips through the quarter mile in 10.7 seconds, and reaches 100mph from rest in around six.

Just 100 SPS models were built. Visually, from the searing red paint to the bold racing #1 on the fairing and the 'Desmoquattro' graphic on the seat, they're indistinguishable from 'ordinary' SP4s.

But look closer. The 17 litre petrol tank is carbon-fibre. The engine differs from the full-on racers only in running a '91-spec Corsa exhaust cam, road transmission and starter motor. If you look carefully, you might spot the Corsa radiator, and the absence of the SP4's fan.

Like the SP4, the Duke has a full 888cc (94 x 64mm), breathing through four desmodromically-controlled valves and two belt-driven cams per cylinder. There's a six-speed gearbox, a dry clutch, and fully-mapped Weber-Marelli fuel injection. The engine breathes through the biggest chokes in the business – 50mm – each with not one, but two injector nozzles.

Unlike the SP4, the crankcases, crankshaft, pistons and inlet cam are pure Corsa. Ditto the free-flowing down-pipes, and the valvegear. At 34mm, the inlet valves are 1mm bigger than the SP4's, with 1mm more lift. The 30mm exhaust valves are also 1mm bigger, with the same lift. Compression is up a point at 12.0:1. The SPS gets its own fuel injection chip – basically with Corsa mapping, but taking account of the air filter. To uprate the SPS into a full-blown works replica, all it needs is a Corsa '92 exhaust cam, airbox and chip. The job is so straightforward that Ducati importers Moto Cinelli put one on the track, in the hands of Michael Rutter.

SPECIFICATION: DUCATI 888SPS	
ENGINE	Liquid-cooled DOHC 8-valve Desmo V-twin
DISPLACEMENT	888cc
HORSEPOWER	120bhp @ 10,500rpm
CARBURETTORS	Programmed fuel injection, 50mm chokes
GEAR BOX	Six speed
FRAME	Tubular steel trellis
WHEELBASE	56.3ins
WEIGHT	403lbs dry
TOP SPEED	165mph

Number '1' on the fairing is no idle boast. This is as close to Doug Polen's world superbikes winner as the well-heeled road rider can hope to get.

Now the SP4 is no slowcoach. The SPS, with 11lbs less weight and nine more horsepower, is everything you'd expect it to be – and more. Unlike more ordinary Ducatis, power feels flat below 6000rpm, then it rockets to the far side of 10,000rpm. The two bikes share the same 15/37 final drive ratio, so their top speeds are similar – on the far side of 160mph. Where the SPS scores is in acceleration.

The chassis is identical to the SP4's – same chrome-molybdenum steel frame, same aluminium swing-arm, same geometry (24°30′ rake, 94mm trail), and the same peerless Öhlins suspension. Pre-load, compression and rebound damping are adjustable at both ends. The 42mm upside-down forks, with 120mm of travel, are supremely good on the brakes. The rear unit, giving 110mm of wheel travel, is everything you'd expect of an Öhlins. Brakes, inevitably, are by Brembo – and *huge*.

With so much torque on tap, this particular Ducati feels twitchier than all the eight-valvers which have gone before. Ride smoothly, particularly when changing gear cranked over, and it behaves. Ride abruptly, and the head can wag in protest. Steering precision is otherwise excellent.

SP4 from which the SPS was developed gave way to this, the SP5 – by any standards also a superbike.

So, if you had one, what would you do? Would you leave the gearing as is, and relish that sensational surge of acceleration? Or gear it up and humiliate 'ordinary' machines like the SP4? The question is probably academic: even at £16,500, all 15 brought into the UK were sold before the brochure's ink was dry.

Lashings of carbon fibre and 'Corsa' race components make the SPS especially super, even by superbike standards.

Ducati 916

'The spread of power is so immense that almost any gear will do.'

To many, Ducati's 916 is not merely a superbike, but *the* Superbike. Part motorcycle, part fantasy, part erotic art, few motorcycles of the past 20 years have aroused such passion amongst the motorcycling public.

Just look at it. Is there such a thing as Repetitive Strain Injury of the desire muscles? There is now. Within nanoseconds of its UK launch in late 1993, a whole generation of bikers had instantly put the 916 top of their lust list. Practically overnight, every one of the 200 destined for Britain in 1994 were sold. And the first 100 due in '95. Even at £11,800 apiece, it seemed cheap.

Not only does the 916 have looks in abundance, it has pedigree. Essentially, it is a racer, with the almost desultory addition of lights and a number plate. It is little more than a spin-off from World Superbike regulations which insist that if you can't find the same frame, engine castings and induction system in the shops, you can't put them on the track, either. For this reason, Honda would probably never have built their RC45 were it not for their Superbike racing ambitions. Ducati, on the other hand, almost certainly would have built the 916 – because they're Italian and Italians are into that sort of thing.

The 916's predecessor, the 888, had already won the World Superbike crown in 1990, '91, '92. Hot off the drawing board, the 916 followed suit, taking Carl Fogarty to memorable victory in the 1994 title chase. By the time you read this, he'll probably have won it again. And if Fogarty doesn't, another 916 almost certainly will.

Despite the leanness of its lines, the 916 is an extraordinarily complex box of tricks. That slim

SPECIFICATION: DUCATI 916	
ENGINE	Liquid-cooled DOHC 8-valve Desmo V-twin
DISPLACEMENT	916cc
HORSEPOWER	114bhp @ 9000rpm
CARBURETTORS	Programmed fuel injection, 50mm chokes
GEAR BOX	Six speed
FRAME	Tubular steel trellis
WHEELBASE	55.5ins
WEIGHT	430lbs dry
TOP SPEED	160mph

Not surprisingly, it was lust at first sight for a generation of bikers when the 916 was first unveiled. No previous machine had embodied quite the same combination of race-bred performance and sensuous good looks as the road-going counterpart of the machine which would take Carl Fogarty to his first World Superbike title.

fairing hides an engine which may 'only' be a twin, the latest in a line of Ducati V-twins dating back to 1972. But the latest Dukes have four valves per cylinder, four camshafts, six gears, liquid-cooling, computer-controlled electronic fuel injection and desmodromic valvegear.

All this advanced technology makes the 916 quite unlike most racing engines. Instead of a diet of pure, giddy revs, the twin pours out irrepressible, visceral urge almost from tickover. Solid, hard power begins as low as 3000rpm, and from 6000-upwards the universe is thrown into reverse. Top speed is a blistering 160mph.

In 955cc Superbike racing trim, the '916' develops the thick end of 150bhp. As a roadster it claims 114bhp at 9000rpm, but feels even stronger, more usable. The spread of power is so immense that almost any gear will do. And the booming roar when downshifting into corners is one of the joys of motorcycling.

The Ducati's chassis, too, is of the highest class. Compared to the 888, the 916 is shorter, more agile, more racer-like. The Japanese Showa suspension offers a huge array of settings, but there is very little wrong with the Duke straight out of the crate. With its short wheelbase and its lively geometry, it is in its element through turns – blindingly fast sweepers and hairpins alike.

Anyone buying the 916 takes custody of a dream as much as reality. As a practical street bike it has its faults, not the least of which is comfort. In a racing crouch – what it was designed for, after all – it fits like a glove. As a tourer, it makes a good plank. This is not a practical motorcycle, and every red-blooded rider in the world should want one.

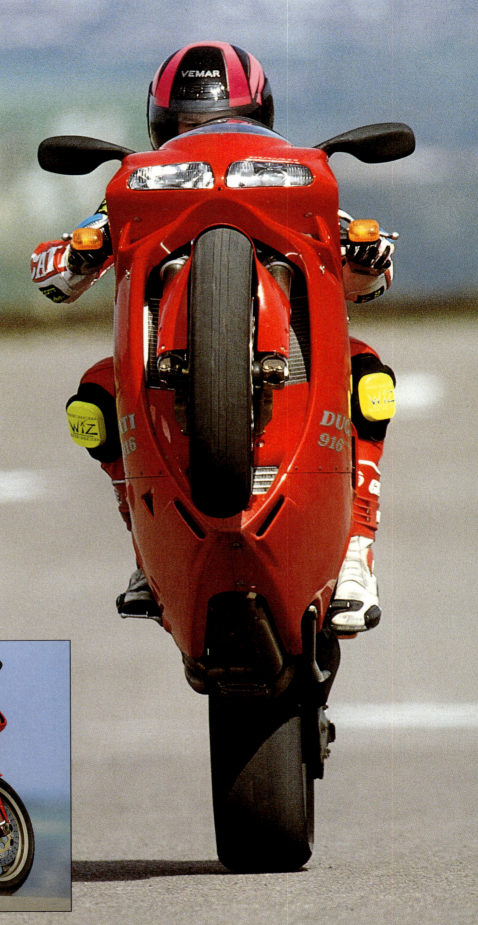

Ducati 900 Superlight

Red, raw and unashamedly singleminded, Ducati's 900 Superlight proved conclusively that a sports bike could provide high performance – not with excessive horsepower but through simplicity, light weight and agile handling. By modern standards the Superlight was only moderately powerful – but it was rapid, exciting and every last millimetre a pure-bred Ducati sportster.

The Superlight was launched in 1992 as a racer, more aggressive relative of the 900SS, which had been introduced in 1989 and revamped to good effect two years later. Essentially the new model was a hard-charging, single-seat version of the SS, complete with reduced weight and numerous other changes intended to cash in on Ducati's early-'90s domination of the World Superbike race series.

Most of the Superlight's 90-degree V-twin engine was derived from the 900SS, which meant it was a 904cc, single overhead camshaft unit with two valves per cylinder and desmodromic valve operation (valves closed positively, instead of by springs). The gearbox remained a six-speed unit; the only transmission difference was a ventilated cover for the Superlight's dry clutch.

The 900SS's pair of 38mm downdraft Mikunis was retained, which helped give an identical claimed peak output of 73bhp at 7000rpm. The Superlight's lack of a pillion seat allowed the free-breathing exhaust pipes to sit higher. At the other end, the new bike gained a front mudguard of lightweight carbon-fibre, instead of the conventional plastic.

In Ducati tradition the Superlight's chassis was based around a tubular steel ladder frame, and featured low-set clip-on handlebars and rearset footrests. Most of the chassis was shared with the 900SS, including the sturdy 41mm upside-down front forks from Showa, and the same Japanese firm's multi-adjustable rear shock, working directly on a cantilever swing-arm.

To that successful format the Superlight added composite wheels with aluminium rims and lightweight magnesium spokes, wearing Michelin's Hi-Sport radial tyres in suitably broad sizes. Brakes

Essentially a lightened version of the Ducati 900SS, the Superlight is a worthy descendant of the first Ducati superbikes of the mid-'seventies — lean, light and uncompromisingly purposeful.

Gutsy V-twin powerplant allows the Superlight to power hard out of bends, almost regardless of gear and revs. Handling is similarly forgiving.

were Brembo's finest: twin 320mm discs up front, gripped by four-piston Gold Line calipers.

As much as its pure performance, it was the Superlight's purposeful attitude and uncompromisingly sporty feel that made the bike so addictive. Its racy red styling, aggressive riding position and rich exhaust note gave a sporty, unmistakably V-twin feel, and the Ducati's blend of gutsy midrange torque, light weight and crisp throttle response made for a wonderfully eager and easy-to-ride machine.

That 73bhp peak output resulted in a top speed of almost 140mph, which could be bettered by several Japanese 750s. But the Ducati's combination of superlightness and broad power delivery meant the V-twin could stay with almost any competition on all but an arrow-straight road. Given a crack of the throttle the Superlight thundered off, remaining reasonably smooth all the way to its 9000rpm redline.

Handling was excellent too, thanks to the Superlight's rigid frame and its collection of top-quality cycle parts. Steering was light and neutral, giving the 388lbs Ducati the feel of a genuine middleweight. The adjustable forks gave a ride that was firm without being harsh, and the firmly sprung rear end was superbly well-controlled, even when being worked hard by the aggressive cornering encouraged by the grip of the fat and sticky rear Hi Sport tyre.

Whether the Superlight's 15lbs weight advantage, compared to the 900SS, was strictly noticeable was debatable, and the two models were certainly very

closely related in performance, as well as specification. The new bike's price was considerably higher, too. But for riders addicted to the speed, style and simplicity of Ducati's two-valves-per-cylinder V-twins, the 900 Superlight was second to none.

SPECIFICATION: DUCATI 900 SUPERLIGHT	
ENGINE	Air/oil-cooled SOHC 4-valve Desmo V-twin
DISPLACEMENT	904cc
HORSEPOWER	73bhp @ 7000rpm
CARBURETTORS	2 x 38mm Mikuni
GEAR BOX	Six speed
FRAME	Tubular steel ladder
WHEELBASE	56ins
WEIGHT	388lbs dry
TOP SPEED	137mph

Despite the fashion for aluminium beam frames, Ducati remain devoted to a steel trellis design, for the simple reason that it works.

Egli Harley-Davidson

'Vibration from the solidly-mounted motor added to the sensation of speed, too.'

Raucous, raw and very, very rare, Fritz Egli's radical reworking of the Harley theme has more than double the power of the original.

Former Swiss racing champion Fritz Egli has been building beautifully engineered bikes around his own chassis for over 25 years. When Egli adapted his traditional steel spine frame to hold a tuned, 1607cc Harley-Davidson V-twin engine, the result was an exciting machine that was outrageous by any standards – and especially those of environment-conscious Switzerland, notorious for its strict limits on motorcycles' power and noise.

Big, basic and muscular, the first Egli Harley, built in 1992, had an aggressive and vaguely classic look, thanks to bodywork fashioned from 1960s-style unpainted aluminium. A huge petrol tank curved over the top of the grey-finished Evolution engine. Large triangular sidepanels ran below a one-and-a-half-person seat. Front and rear mudguards were also made from bare alloy sheet.

The frame consisted of a main steel spine, which doubled as the oil reservoir, plus narrower tubes that held the motor in a conventional twin cradle. Egli himself built numerous parts, including the 38mm diameter front forks and their yokes. At the rear, the triangulated steel swing-arm worked a single, multi-adjustable White Power shock absorber.

The motor was far from standard, having been built by Egli to incorporate a long list of tuning parts including Cosworth pistons, Carrillo rods and Manley valves. Plumbed with a 36mm Mikuni carburettor and an Egli-made exhaust system, the result was an increase in the V-twin's capacity from 1340cc to a massive 1607cc, raising peak output to 120bhp at 5500rpm.

When the big Harley burst into life, it did so with enough noise to start an avalanche. The view from the pilot's seat was intimidating. There was a long stretch across the alloy tank to adjustable clip-on bars that were set low and wide. Standard Harley clocks perched above the protruding fork-tops, the tacho needle flicking across the dial with every blip of the throttle.

Riding the Egli Harley confirmed that it was no docile modern sportster but a big, old-fashioned bruiser of a bike that needed a firm hand to give of its best. Its wheelbase was compact by Harley standards, at 60ins. But conservative steering geometry, an 18-inch front wheel and a high centre of gravity meant a good deal of effort was needed to change direction.

Suspension was firm and worked well on smooth roads, the forks feeling reassuringly rigid and the well-damped rear unit keeping the back end under control. Despite its much-increased output, the engine was as tractable as any Harley motor. Crack open the throttle, and the bike hurtled forward to the accompaniment of an increasingly frenzied barrage of sound from the exhaust.

Vibration from the solidly-mounted motor added to the sensation of speed, too. Below 3000rpm the big V-twin was smooth, giving a relaxed feel up to 60mph in top gear. But the vibes arrived at that figure and increased steadily. Although the Egli stormed past 100mph on the way to a top speed of about 130mph, fast cruising was best limited to short bursts.

Rubber-mounting the engine would have been one solution – but, as Fritz Egli pointed out, much of the bike's appeal came from its raw feel, to which the untamed V-twin lump was a major contributor. At least there was no pretence with an Egli Harley. What you saw was a big, old-fashioned V-twin brute of a machine, and that was precisely what you got. Plenty of sports bikes were faster and more agile than the Egli. Few were more thrilling to ride.

SPECIFICATION: EGLI HARLEY-DAVIDSON	
ENGINE	Air-cooled pushrod OHV 45-degree V-twin
DISPLACEMENT	1607cc
HORSEPOWER	120bhp @ 5500rpm
CARBURETTORS	36mm Mikuni
GEAR BOX	Five speed
FRAME	Steel main spine and duplex cradle
WHEELBASE	60ins
WEIGHT	520lbs dry
TOP SPEED	130mph

130mph and no fairing gives the rider two choices: tuck in, or get blown away.

Steel spine frame, bespoke forks and White Power suspension still struggle to cope with a machine weighing well over 500lbs.

Harley-Davidson Dyna Glide

'The essence of
any Harley is
that pounding
V-twin beat.'

The Dyna Glide features Harley-Davidson's latest chassis, which Harley themselves proudly claim is the result of computer-aided design (CAD). But it's a far cry from the exotic aluminium beam frames favoured by the latest Japanese race replicas. This one's steel, good ol' US steel, a direct spiritual descendant of an earlier generation of American iron horses.

Seemingly sculpted from solid billets of Milwaukee metal, Harleys spurn 'crotch rocket' styling in favour of timeless V-twin appeal. Well-spaced fork legs mark this as the 'Wide Glide' version.

But the frame is, in its modest way, a new departure for Harley-D as they progress ever-so-cautiously into the future. First seen on the 1991 Sturgis model, it features a refinement of the system of rubber engine mounting previously fitted to Glide and Low Rider models. And for the first time, it is possible for a normal person to ride a Harley at sustained speed without going numb from the wrists down.

Purists might frown. The essence of any Harley is that pounding V-twin beat. Unlike the anodyne whirr of Japanese multis, you're *supposed* to feel it. Dyna Glide's endeavour to offer the best of both worlds: you can tell there's 80 cubic inches of Milwaukee muscle down there, all right, but it doesn't put your circulation in a sling.

To ride, these are the smoothest Hogs yet, by a margin. Even sensitive souls will use power outside the Evolution engine's hitherto rev-range without worrying that the entire bike's about to fall to bits. Now you can happily ride at low revs where other Hogs quake and shudder. Or at high revs where your fillings used to be in danger of shaking out. Without laying a hand on the engine, rubber mounting has effectively widened the big Vee's powerband.

Harley themselves bill the Dynas as 'combining '70s Low Rider looks with the handling and rubber-isolated ride of today's Low Riders'. Both standard, 'Low Rider' and 'Wide Glide' models have been produced, the latter with the fork legs widely spaced. These are lean, low machines by Harley standards, styled according to whatever passes for grace in Milwaukee.

The rest, as is Harley's way, is largely in the hands of the cosmetic engineers. Using just two engines (Sporters of 883 & 1200cc, plus the 1340cc twin), and a handful of frame designs, the Milwaukee company typically produces around 20 models per year. It follows that many of the differences are cosmetic, and there are truly only four types of Harley: Sportsters, Low Riders, Softails and Glides. Dyna Glides are essentially a variation of the Low Rider theme.

This is precisely the point. Whilst owners of European and Japanese sports machines might discuss the number of valves per cylinder, or the thousands of suspension options available, Harley owners are interested in style. If it's paint, badging, chrome or tassels, Harley can supply it from a bewildering accessory list. And if they can't, an entire industry of custom goodies manufacturers will be happy to oblige.

Equally, whilst outright performance is rarely at the top of any Harley owner's shopping list, mild performance options are popular. Again, there's a Harley catalogue of bolt-on 'Screaming Eagle' parts.

Such are the number of variables that it's impossible to describe in detail how any particular model performs: on the whim of the stylists different Dyna Glides, for instance, feature one or two front disc brakes. So some stop, and some don't. Dyna Wide Glide's have poor ground clearance, even by Harley standards. Others are adequate, just about.

Inescapably, functionality is not the point. It's how a Harley looks that makes it Super. Beauty might be in the eye of the beholder, but nothing turns heads quite like a Hog.

SPECIFICATION:	HARLEY-DAVIDSON DYNA GLIDE
ENGINE	Air-cooled OHV 45-degree V-twin
DISPLACEMENT	1340cc
HORSEPOWER	55bhp @ 5000rpm
CARBURETTORS	40mm Keihin
GEAR BOX	Five speed
FRAME	Tubular steel twin cradle
WHEELBASE	65.5in
WEIGHT	599lb
TOP SPEED	105mph

Upper digits of speedo are redundant, but on a Hog it's style, not speed, that counts.

Unmistakably 'born in the USA', but modern rubber-mounting of the engine insulates the rider from the shuddering twin's customary vibes.

Harley-Davidson Electra Glide

The Electra Glide has to be one of the most famous names in motorcycling. Ask anyone to name a make and model of motorcycle and the chances are they'll say Harley-Davidson Electra Glide. Immortalised by the film *Electra Glide in Blue*, and by the California Highway Patrol, the Electra Glide is the archetypal American superbike.

The Electra Glide has been around for 30 years, and has remained pretty much unchanged during that time. Harley-Davidsons aren't renowned for their speed or sporting prowess, and the Electra Glide is no exception. Using a large-capacity but low-revving V-twin engine, the Electra Glide is built for comfort rather than speed.

The engine is something of a curiosity in the motorcycle world these days – people just don't build 1340cc air-cooled push-rod V-twins anymore. With increasingly stringent noise and emissions regulations being put in place by governments around the world, the future of the traditional Harley engine looks rather bleak. But until the day arrives when they can't get through the homologation procedures, the big twins will continue to delight their fans.

Harley-Davidsons have been described as being as high-tech as a mangle, and although that is somewhat overstating the case, the appeal of Harleys is their simplicity. That, and their classic

'Undoubtedly gorgeous-looking machines, Harleys have become a cult icon.'

Possibly the biggest item of designer jewellery ever created, the Electra Glide legend rumbles on and on.

The wheels of choice for film stars and rock legends, but the 'Glide is also the Stateside tourer *par excellence*.

good looks. Undoubtedly gorgeous-looking machines, Harleys have become a cult icon. Not all that long ago the Harley was the mount of the outlaw biker, but these days the Harley rider is more likely to be a stockbroker, film star or rock legend. Harleys have become the chic and expensive playthings of the rich and famous.

So what is the Electra Glide like? The engine is a vast unit, heavily over-engineered and built to last a life-time. Although it displaces 1340cc it produces a meagre 55bhp, allowing the Electra Glide to rumble to a top speed of around 110mph. That's not what you'd call fast, but the engine is blessed with an abundance of torque that means you put it in top gear and allow the motor to chug away in its own leisurely way.

The thing to remember about Harleys is they were designed for use in the USA, where 65mph is as fast as you can go and where the distances are huge. For this reason the Electra Glide is designed to cover ground slowly but effortlessly. Unlike machines such as the Honda Gold Wing, which bristle with state-of-the-art electrical gizmos, the Electra Glide relies on soft suspension, a plush seat, and a low-revving engine to make it a fine long-distance tourer. And a very accomplished tourer it is – it will cover 200 miles without having to stop for fuel, and when you do stop you aren't suffering the aches and pains experienced with some other touring machines.

Harleys have never had good brakes, high-tech suspension, or any of the other things the

Japanese, British, German or Italian motorcycle manufacturers use to make their machine better than anyone else's. Instead, Harleys are built to a competent level and the Harley image and name does the rest. The fact that they look fantastic and are very desirable means that Harley-Davidson sell every one they make without any effort at all. The Electra Glide might not be fast, it might not be powerful, but it is certainly one of the most stylish and prestigious superbikes around today.

Only something this big could make 1340cc of air-cooled twin appear dainty.

SPECIFICATION: HARLEY-DAVIDSON ELECTRA GLIDE	
ENGINE	Air-cooled OHV 45-degree V-twin
DISPLACEMENT	1340cc
HORSEPOWER	55bhp @ 5000rpm
CARBURETTORS	40mm Keihin
GEAR BOX	Five speed
FRAME	Steel double-cradle
WHEELBASE	62.9ins
WEIGHT	741lbs dry
TOP SPEED	110mph

Harley-Davidson Heritage Softail

'Not for Harley the headlong race for performance.'

Nostalgia, as they say, isn't what it used to be. It's better. For this, ladies and gentlemen, is Retro-tech. It is Harley-Davidson's shatteringly successful attempt to sell back to the motorcycling public those dreamy days of the 'fifties when the sun always shone and the Platters presided over a million teenage romances.

Not for Harley the headlong race for performance. Of overhead camshafts, they have none. Two valves per cylinder is all you get, and liquid-cooling is strictly for cars. What you get instead is style, American-style, in huge imposing motorcycles deliberately engineered to ape a bygone age: Retro-tech.

Although the Glide range has now evolved into something distinct (see page 36), the Heritage Softail is not unlike the original Glide, the Hydra-Glide of 1949. This was the first Milwaukee machine to feature telescopic forks, and the Softail's are shrouded to emulate the earlier design.

Glides didn't boast swing-arm rear suspension until the Duo-Glide of 1958. A cursory inspection of any Softail suggests that it, too, is a pre-'58 design. But what the designers have done is style a rear suspension which looks 'hardtail', but is in fact fully sprung. A pair of damper units reside discreetly under the gearbox as though ashamed to own up to the 1990s. This is 'Softail' and, like most things Harley, even the name is copyright.

Between '49-style forks and the *appearance* of no rear suspension is slung the classic Harley V-twin. Like the chassis, on first examination it could have been built pretty well any time between 1920 and the present. But yet again, appearances are deceptive. This is a 1340cc 'Evolution' unit, dating from 1985. Modernisation has improved reliability, without sacrificing the V-twin's classic charm.

All these things the Heritage has in common with the rest of the Softail range – the 'standard' Softail Custom and the Fat Boy. The Springer Softail goes even further down the retro route in wearing forks which mimic '30s girders. All are massive machines – the lightest is 617lbs – with distinctly modest power outputs, and the power-to-weight of a not very sporting car. Cruising, not scratching, is where Softails are at.

So riding any Harley is more a spiritual experience than an adrenaline-soaked thrill. The Heritage Softail, arguably the biggest fashion accessory in the world, takes this to extremes. It rolls around amiably on its ponderously fat tyres, vibrates like mad at any sort of revs and changes gear only in its own good time.

Since, unlike Glides, Softail engines are not rubber-mounted, vibration is acute at high revs. You're never left in any doubt that the shuddering lump under the petrol tank is a real engine producing prodigious torque at low revs, the two-wheeled equivalent of generations of Detroit V-eights. This, more than anything else, is a Harley's soul.

The rear suspension, meanwhile, is better than it looks without actually being much good. Despite the constraints inherent in the styling, Softails in fact boast more rear suspension travel – 4.06in – than any other models in the Harley range. But hit something hard, and you'd better hope your vertebrae are in good shape. Braking is similarly feeble by current standards. It is actually possible to lock a Softail

Despite rumours to the contrary, with the Softail, nostalgia definitely *is* what it used to be — or as near as Harley can make it. And very lucratively so.

front wheel, but you need a helluva fright to work up the necessary energy. Like all Harleys, you use plenty of rear brake to slow down.

But slow and stately is the point. Legends, after all, are not to be hurried.

SPECIFICATION:	HARLEY-DAVIDSON HERITAGE SOFTAIL
ENGINE	Air-cooled OHV 45-degree V-twin
DISPLACEMENT	1340cc
HORSEPOWER	55bhp @ 5000rpm
CARBURETTORS	40mm Keihin
GEAR BOX	Five speed
FRAME	Tubular steel twin cradle
WHEELBASE	62.5in
WEIGHT	710lb
TOP SPEED	105mph

Cruisin' is what Harleys do best, whether loping across the American Prairies or ambling along English country lanes.

Lazy, low-revving 'Evolution' engine has deservedly banished the reputation Harleys once had for unreliability.

Honda CB1000

....

*I*n an attempt, a few years ago, to lure the ageing and lapsed motorcyclist back on to two wheels, many of the motorbike manufacturers adopted what is known as the *Retro* look.

Time was when all superbikes were gas-guzzling monsters unadorned by acres of fibreglass bodywork. A superbike was a machine with a very powerful engine, two wheels and a seat. They required nerves of steel and a will of iron to tame, and they had a brutish appeal almost totally absent from most modern superbikes . . . except for the retro ones.

The retro superbikes are designed to appeal to those who are old enough to remember unfaired muscle-bikes the first time round – those who rode bikes in the '70s and who aren't now limber enough to squeeze themselves aboard a state-of-the-art race-replica. The born-again biker is the target market for these bikes, and one of the best examples of these retro machines is the Honda CB1000.

Using a de-tuned engine from a Honda CBR1000F, the CB1000 harks back to the days of the CB1100 and the CB900. The water-cooled, double overhead cam, 16-valve, in-line four cylinder engine is a far cry from the air-cooled eight-valve engines of the '70s, but it is the focal point of this superbike. Pumping out 100bhp at 8500rpm the CB1000 has a top speed of around 140mph.

The 'Big 'Un' is the he-man of modern superbikes, demanding an uncompromisingly muscular style for this sort of action.

The engine is capable of producing a lot more power than it actually does, but Honda have tuned it for low and mid-range output, and brute acceleration, rather than top speed. This is because without a fairing on it, the CB1000 is a struggle to ride at speeds over 120mph. So it might as well be tuned for eyeball-popping acceleration instead.

In the USA muscle-bikes such as Yamaha's V-Max have proved to be very popular, combining brute power with an upright and unfaired riding position. The retro bike is a similar animal, offering old-fashioned good looks with straight-line acceleration that is the envy of the sportscar world.

In Japan the CB1000 is called the CB1000 Big One, and with good reason – this is one *BIG* motorcycle. Weighing in at 520lbs dry, with a seat height of 31.5ins, and with a wheelbase of 60.6ins, the CB1000 is a massive machine. It's not in the

same league as bikes such as the Gold Wing or the Harley tourers, but compared to modern sportsbikes the CB1000 is massive. Anyone without a 32-inch inside leg measurement and the upper body strength of Arnold Schwarzenegger is going to have trouble manoeuvring this machine at walking pace.

But once you get it moving, the CB1000 doesn't feel quite as ponderous as you might think. The acceleration is awesome, rattling off standing-quarters in the 11-second bracket and laying 50-yard strips of rubber on the road behind if you give it all it's got. And even through the turns the Honda's steel cradle frame and traditional suspension (non-adjustable 43mm telescopic forks at the front and a pair of Showa shocks adjustable for preload only at the rear) keep the bike handling well. The CB1000 isn't going to win many races, but it actually handles considerably better than you'd expect from a bike that weighs this much and comes with a relatively low-tech chassis and suspension.

But the real appeal of the CB1000 is its brutish but linear power delivery and its traditional good looks. It is the essence of the retro look, and that look seems to be here to stay.

Once, all bikes looked roughly like this. But look closely and you'll see lashings of '90s technology lurking under that '70s silhouette.

SPECIFICATION: HONDA CB1000	
ENGINE	Water-cooled DOHC 16-valve in-line four
DISPLACEMENT	998cc
HORSEPOWER	101bhp @ 8500rpm
CARBURETTORS	4 x 34mm Keihin
GEAR BOX	Five speed
FRAME	Tubular steel duplex cradle
WHEELBASE	60.6ins
WEIGHT	520lbs dry
TOP SPEED	140mph

'The acceleration is awesome, rattling off standing-quarters in the 11-second bracket.'

Honda CBR900RR Fireblade

....

*T*he Fireblade is simply the superbike by which all others are currently judged. At the cutting-edge of superbike technology, the Fireblade combines superlative performance with light weight and peerless handling to create a bike that many have tried to imitate but none has equalled.

Motorcycle manufacturers love to announce 'revolutionary new concepts' in motorcycle design, but realistically few of them ever come up with any such thing. Yet the Fireblade is one such machine. Launched in 1992, it re-wrote the rule book for performance motorcycles, combining litre bike power in a package the size and weight of a 600. Overnight, the rest of the supersport litre bike class became dinosaurs. What previously was thought to be the pinnacle of motorcycle performance was suddenly rendered obsolete.

So what makes the Fireblade so special? Very simply, it is the combination of a powerful engine in a small, lightweight machine, fitted with state-of-the-art suspension and brakes. The engine itself is nothing exceptional, being a very familiar water-cooled DOHC 16-valve in-line four putting out 125bhp – pretty much the industry standard for a 1000cc machine.

The chassis is an aluminium-alloy beam, again an industry standard in the supersports category, with a pair of hefty 45mm telescopic forks at the front and a multi-adjustable rising-rate monoshock at the back. Interestingly, Honda ignored the current trend for fitting inverted telescopic forks and a 17-inch front wheel to the Fireblade, instead opting for ordinary telescopic forks and a 16-inch wheel. Brakes are a pair of 296mm discs at the front

Britain's best-selling superbike packs a heavyweight punch into a middleweight parcel. When launched in 1992, it re-wrote the rules.

16 inch front wheel and hyper-fast geometry make the 'Blade quicker into turns than any comparable machine.

'The nature of the Fireblade means that this is not a bike for the faint-hearted or for the touring motorcyclist.'

with four-piston calipers, and a single 240mm disc at the back.

Looking at the specification sheet of the Fireblade, it's hard to work out quite why this is such an exceptional motorcycle. The sum of the parts doesn't seem to add up to anything more than what is on offer from the other manufacturers of superbikes, yet in use the Fireblade stands head and shoulders above everything except the priciest hand-built exotica from Italy.

On the road the Fireblade is so light and so nimble it feels like a race-bred middleweight, yet it packs the punch of a bike from the heavyweight division. The steering response is razor-sharp and allows the Fireblade to be flicked through corners at tremendous speed and with absolute precision. Although the Fireblade may not be the fastest bike on the roads (a top-speed of 165mph is a good 10mph down on machines like the Kawasaki ZZ-R1100), it is almost certainly the fastest bike point-to-point. The ease with which it corners, brakes and accelerates means that off the motorway there's nothing to touch it (except another Fireblade).

The nature of the Fireblade means that this is not a bike for the faint-hearted or for the touring motorcyclist. It is cramped and not at all comfortable, nor is it very practical. But for pure, hedonistic motorcycling at the very edge of the performance envelope there isn't much that comes close.

The Fireblade has raised superbike performance to a level now where the only limits are those of the rider rather than those of the machine. Motorcycle manufacturers will continue to produce better and better machines, but the Fireblade will be remembered as the bike that brought perfection to the masses, and at an affordable price.

SPECIFICATION: HONDA FIREBLADE	
ENGINE	Liquid-cooled DOHC 16-valve in-line four
DISPLACEMENT	893cc
HORSEPOWER	124bhp @ 11000rpm
CARBURETTORS	4 x 38mm Keihin CV
GEAR BOX	Six speed
FRAME	Aluminium-alloy twin beam
WHEELBASE	55.3ins
WEIGHT	407lbs dry
TOP SPEED	165mph

Searing acceleration makes keeping the front wheel down the hardest trick in the Fireblade book.

Honda GL1500 Gold Wing

'On the open road the Gold Wing performs faultlessly, as long as you never forget it weighs 800lbs and isn't designed as a sportsbike.'

When it comes to sheer size, superbikes don't come any bigger than Honda's GL1500 Gold Wing. This leviathan of the two-wheeled world is the ultimate in motorcycling comfort, designed solely to transport two people in as much style and luxury as is possible.

The Gold Wing has been around for two decades, during which time it has evolved from a fairly basic naked tourer into an everything-but-the-kitchen-sink machine for the discerning traveller. It began life as a 1000cc flat-four, grew to an 1100cc flat-four, a 1200cc flat-four, and finally into a 1500cc flat-six.

Yes, six cylinders power this mighty beast, producing 98bhp at 5200rpm and a massive 110ft/lb of torque at 4000rpm. Despite weighing in at a hefty 800lbs dry, the 'Wing is capable of a top speed of 130mph, although it takes its time getting there.

But top speed isn't what the Gold Wing is about. Smooth, effortless power delivery, luggage-carrying capacity, and supreme comfort, are what the Gold Wing is all about. And it is justly famous for achieving its purpose. The barn-door-like fairing is large enough to keep the wind and rain off the rider (although internal vents in the fairing allow you to direct cooling air at yourself when the weather gets hot). The saddle is a masterpiece of the furniture-makers art, coddling the behinds of rider and pillion, and adding to the almost total absence of vibrations from the engine to give the smoothest ride known to motorcycling.

Further to enhance the comfort and quality of ride, an on-board air-compressor allows the rider to pump up the rear suspension, and the adjustable

windscreen allows riders of any height the optimum view of the road ahead. Cruise-control is a prerequisite on this kind of bike (designed, as it is, primarily for the US market where speeds are low but sustainable for hours on end), and the Gold Wing has an effective and easy-to-use one.

But the *pièce de résistance* is the Gold Wing's sound system. The radio-cassette player is an amazing piece of technology that allows you to listen to your favourite music as you cruise the highways. Even at three-figure speeds the stereo system is clearly audible thanks to the sensor that automatically adjusts the volume to compensate for ambient wind noise.

When it comes to transporting your belongings, the Gold Wing is similarly impressive. The panniers and top-box will swallow huge amounts of luggage, and the top-box even boasts an interior light and vanity mirror!

On the open road the Gold Wing performs faultlessly, as long as you never forget it weighs 800lbs and isn't designed as a sportsbike. Fully-loaded the 'Wing will cruise all day at 90mph while you and your passenger sit comfortably behind the huge fairing listening to your favourite radio programme. With a range of over 200 miles from a tankful of fuel the 'Wing can cover 1000 miles in a day with ease, and still leave the rider fresh enough to do the same again the next day. And the day after that.

And that is the sole purpose of the Gold Wing, to make travelling by motorcycle as comfortable and pleasant as possible. It doesn't offer adrenaline-pumping speed or svelte good looks, it just makes touring a uniquely majestic experience.

SPECIFICATION: HONDA GOLD WING	
ENGINE	Water-cooled SOHC horizontally-opposed flat-six
DISPLACEMENT	1520cc
HORSEPOWER	98bhp @ 5200rpm
CARBURETTORS	2 x 33mm Keihn
GEAR BOX	Five speed
FRAME	Steel double-cradle
WHEELBASE	67ins
WEIGHT	798lbs dry
TOP SPEED	130mph

More dials and gizmos than IBM's latest, the 'Wing offers creature comforts few living rooms can equal.

The only 'six' still in production, the low-tuned Boxer engine offers effortless torque at almost any revs.

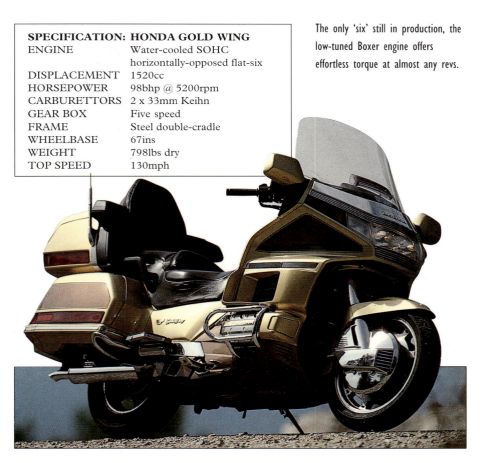

Honda NR750

·····················

The Honda NR750 is possibly the ultimate superbike. It may not be the fastest, and it may not be the best, but it is arguably the best looking, undoubtedly the most technologically advanced, and unquestionably the most expensive.

What makes the NR750 so special is the amazing high-technology it boasts. It is Honda's way of proving how clever they are, corporate muscle-flexing by a company who wanted to prove that they build quality as well as quantity. Space-age engineering is packed into every cranny of the NR, making it a unique and fascinating machine. But at £36,500 each (and Honda only built 700 of them) you'd expect it to be rare. When it costs five times more than the same company's flag-ship sportsbike, the NR750 would have to be something a bit out of the ordinary.

What's most special about the NR750 is its engine. The NR is clever in many respects, but the it is the engine that sets it apart from any other

motorcycle. This liquid-cooled V4 motor uses oval pistons, no less than *eight* valves per cylinder and features a highly sophisticated fuel-injection system. A 32-valve fuel-injected V4 750 is an astonishing feat of engineering, and one which allows Honda to produce a lot of power from a relatively small package.

Each of the two cylinder banks has double overhead cams. Each piston (they are actually oblong shaped, but with rounded-off corners, rather than purely oval) has two con-rods, two spark-plugs and eight valves. Why all this high-technology? Engines using lots of valves, all opening and closing quickly, can rev higher than ones with fewer valves. With a rev limit of 15,000rpm and an advanced fuel-injection system, the NR750 produces an impressive 125bhp (although pre-production prototypes were capable of 140bhp and the racing bike on which the NR is based was making more than 160bhp).

'Even the windscreen is titanium-coated and costs more than most people earn in a month.'

The most expensive production motorcycle ever built, even the NR's flaming red paint pushes the frontiers of science.

Biggest handling drawback for the NR is the sheer weight of all that technology, yet this is still a precision projectile on both road and track.

But there's more to the NR750 than oval-piston technology. The aluminium-alloy chassis is a work of art, combining strength and rigidity with lightness, and the NR's suspension is the best money can buy. At the front the NR features massive inverted Showa forks and at the back it uses Honda's fiendishly clever single-sided swingarm developed for fast wheel changes in endurance racing.

But most breath-taking of all is the body-work, an impressive mixture of carbon-fibre and fibreglass that costs more than the total price of any other mass-production motorcycle. Even the NR's windscreen is titanium-coated and costs more than most people earn in a month. The styling of the bodywork is sleek and seductive, the lines beautiful and the finish higher quality than anything seen before from a 'mass-produced' motorcycle.

As far as performance goes, the NR is good rather than exceptional. There are plenty of other motorbikes that will accelerate faster and reach a higher top speed, but the NR750 is one of the best handling bikes on the road, capable of going from 0-60mph in under four seconds and reaching a top speed of 160mph.

The NR750 is so expensive and exclusive that most people will never see one, let alone come across one on a public road. Which is a shame because it is undoubtedly the best looking and most exciting production motorcycle ever made.

SPECIFICATION: HONDA NR750	
ENGINE	Liquid-cooled DOHC 32 valve oval-piston V4
DISPLACEMENT	748cc
HORSEPOWER	125bhp @ 14000rpm
CARBURETTORS	Electronic fuel injection
GEAR BOX	Six speed
FRAME	Aluminium-alloy twin beam
WHEELBASE	56.4ins
WEIGHT	480lbs dry
TOP SPEED	160mph

Honda RC30

·····························

The Honda RC30 marked a huge leap forward in Japanese motorcycle design. It was the first Japanese bike to rival the beauty and build quality previously the domain of exotic specialists like Bimota. When it hit the market in 1988 the press were in danger of running out of superlatives. And dealers soon ran out of bikes to sell to the well-heeled enthusiasts who queued up to spend twice the price of a Suzuki GSX-R on the most talked-about bike for years.

And the talk was certainly no exaggeration. The RC30 combined the light weight, quick steering and fantastic rider feedback of a race bike with excellent ride quality, reliability and perfectly stable behaviour on even the most indifferent road surface.

The RC30 – also called the VFR750R, but everyone referred to it by its factory code name – was based on the all-conquering full-factory RVF750 Endurance and F1 bike. When F1 gave way to World Superbikes, one-off bikes like the RVF were no longer eligible, so the RC was designed from the start as a limited edition road bike, intended to sell just enough to qualify for World Superbikes. Crucial parts – such as chassis, engine casings and carbs – can't be changed under WSB rules, so they needed to be ready to race. In other areas, Honda were free to concentrate on making the RC30 reliable and user-friendly for the road, knowing that those parts could be changed for racing if necessary.

The RC's V-four is a superb road engine. It's smooth, extremely powerful and very reliable. It's also instantly recognisable – you can't mistake the sound or feel of a Honda V-four, whether you're sitting on a standard RC30 blipping the throttle, or sitting by the side of the TT course listening to a

The RC30 was the first superbike truly to be – like this one – equally at home on the race track as on the street. Two world superbike titles for Honda and Fred Merkl can't be wrong.

tuned example on full throttle. The RC has a rich droning exhaust note that never really sounds as though it's working hard. On the road, it probably isn't – even first gear on the RC's close-ratio box is enough to take you to 80mph, so full load in top gear isn't something the RC has to put up with very often.

On the track of course, hard work is what it's all about. A full factory race kit was available from the start – containing everything from modified pistons to new camshafts and crankshafts – as well as kits from the many independent tuners who brought their skills to bear on its complex V-four engine. And the RC30 was born to race. It raised the stakes in the fledgling World Superbike Championships, dominated the demanding Isle of Man TT course and became the bike to have if you wanted to get anywhere in World Endurance. It would be a long time before the other manufacturers caught up.

Visually, the RC shouts its race credentials with its single seat, its smooth, uncompromising lines and its single-sided swing arm at the rear. The latter was designed, like the quick-change mechanisms on the front forks, to waste the minimum time on pit

stops in 24-hour endurance races. For the road it has no real function except to look good – and it certainly does that! Hidden away above it, though, is one of the most perfectly set-up suspension systems ever fitted to a road bike. It tracks over bumps as though they don't exist, and it would take a racetrack to make it misbehave. The forks, too, are well set-up – they may not be fashionable inverted types, but it's the quality that counts.

It's a testimony to the excellence of its design that even now, eight years after its launch, the RC30 is still capable of top ten finishes at the TT, and it's still a stunning bike to ride on the road.

Based upon the legendary factory RVF750, the RC30 began a game of superbike leap-frog which has brought unprecedented riches to the 750cc division – with plenty more, surely, to come.

SPECIFICATION: HONDA RC30	
ENGINE	Water-cooled DOHC 16valve V-four
DISPLACEMENT	748cc
HORSEPOWER	112bhp @ 12,500rpm
CARBURETTORS	4 x 35mm Keihin
GEAR BOX	Six speed
FRAME	Aluminium twin spar
WHEELBASE	55.5ins
WEIGHT	408lbs
TOP SPEED	159mph

'The RC has a rich droning exhaust note that never really sounds as though it's working hard.'

Honda RC45

....

This is very much more than a motorcycle. This is Honda's attempt to wrest world superbike dominance back from Ducati and Kawasaki. The result simply bristles with high technology.

Honda's RC30 was a tough act to follow. It had firmly established itself as one of the all-time great race bikes, and was also a favourite amongst discerning (and well-off) road riders. But by 1993 it had reached the end of its development as far as the increasingly competitive World Superbike Championship was concerned.

Honda still had the exotic works RVF750 race bikes – similar in basic design to the RC30, but representing development work worth millions of dollars. But now the World Endurance series and the Isle of Man TT were to be held under Superbike rules, and the RVF would no longer be eligible.

Honda's answer was to base a new road bike on the RVF, specifically built to win at World Superbike level. Like the RC30, it would be a no-expense-spared, limited production model, and race kits would be available from day one.

It was called the RVF750R, but it's known everywhere by its factory code name – the RC45.

Superficially, it was clearly closely related to the RC30, with its twin spar alloy frame, V-four engine,

single-sided swing arm – even a similar paint scheme. But not a single part is interchangeable between the two.

Superbike rules allow scope for changing engine internals, suspension parts, exhausts and wheels, but they don't allow a complete change of fuel system. This was one of the main reasons the RC30 lost its competitive edge – its carburettors were simply no longer up to the job. With the RC45, Honda took the plunge and fitted an electronic fuel injection system. In terms of pure peak power there's probably little advantage in an injection system, but it simplifies the job of altering the fuelling characteristics to suit different atmospheric conditions or engine set-ups. Instead of dismantling a bank of carburettors to change the jets (notoriously difficult with a complex engine layout like the RC's), all a mechanic has to do is alter the settings on an easily-accessible control box.

Racers and road riders alike queued up to place their orders for the new bike – after all, the RC30 had been superb, so what would its replacement be like? Some road riders, in particular, were disappointed. On the road, the RC45 has no real advantage over the RC30. This is partly because the RC30 had already set such high standards: although the RC45 is faster, has better brakes and suspension and more low-down power, there simply isn't anywhere that an average rider can exploit its advantages. The RC45 operates on a plane of efficiency that doesn't mesh very well with speed limits, blind corners and traffic travelling 100mph slower then the RC45 wants to go.

On the race track, too, the RC45 took a while to come good. It was quickly on the pace and running near the front in Superbikes, and was often fastest through the speed traps, but never seemed to translate that into a winning performance. The Ducati 916 had a weight advantage over the Honda

which gave it better acceleration out of corners. The ZXR750 Kawasaki had the benefit of several years' continuous development. The Honda had a handling problem – lack of traction out of corners. It was eventually traced to the rear suspension linkage, which was quickly revised. Soon the RC45 started to notch up race success, with victory in the prestigious Suzuka Eight Hour race and its first World Superbike success in the hands of Aaron Slight at Albacete in Spain. The RC had already proved its reliability with two victories at the Le Mans 24-hour race, and had taken over from the factory RVF as king of the Mountain Course at the Isle of Man. But, two seasons into its Superbike career, it still can't match those damn Ducatis.

Despite persistent problems on the race track, RC45 handling is utterly beyond reproach on the road.

SPECIFICATION: HONDA RC45	
ENGINE	Water-cooled DOHC 16-valve, 90° V-four
DISPLACEMENT	749cc
HORSEPOWER	118bhp @ 12,000rpm
CARBURETTORS	PGM FI fuel injection
GEAR BOX	Six speed
FRAME	Aluminium twin spar
WHEELBASE	55.5ins
WEIGHT	417lbs dry
TOP SPEED	165mph

Kawasaki 1100 Zephyr

································

Kawasaki were the first Japanese company to look back on their own history for inspiration when designing new bikes. The result was the Zephyr range, introduced in 1991. The 550 and 750 Zephyrs, both styled like Kawasaki's muscle bikes of the 'seventies, sold well to people who were attracted to the simplicity and spirit of a 'seventies bike, but who wanted 'nineties reliability and a warranty. The 'retro' movement was born. But what real muscle bike fans wanted was the true successor to the hairy-chested Z1 and the later Z1000.

They got it in 1992, with the Zephyr 1100.

In stark contrast to the firm's other flagship 1100, the ZZ-R, the Zephyr is a model of simplicity, consisting of little more than an engine, two wheels and just enough other equipment to hold them together. Visually, the Zephyr takes its styling cues from the Z1. But not a standard Z1. What Kawasaki did was to build a bike that incorporated all the modifications people made to their old Zeds as technology moved on and parts from later bikes became available.

So, the Zephyr has an alloy box-section swinging arm at the rear, operating remote reservoir twin shocks with adjustable damping. At the front, huge twin brake discs and four-piston calipers from the ZZ-R1100 are a far cry from the Z1's single front disc and single-piston caliper. Alloy wheels fitted with wide, sticky tyres complete the picture.

The result of all this attention to the running gear is a bike that's superbly balanced, with plenty of ground clearance for fast back-road riding, and impeccable low-speed manners. The Zephyr is a

Kawasaki were the first to exploit the Retro concept, and after-market suppliers have been happy to leap into the same niche. The Cyclone reflects a growing trend towards customised variants.

Tracing its mechanical ancestry all the way back over 20 years to the Z1, the biggest Zephyr's handling is not for the faint-hearted.

heavy bike, but it carries its weight low, making for good manoeuvrability The low seat and upright riding position help here, too – a relief for many after the race crouch of most modern sports bikes.

But it's the engine that gives the Zephyr its real character. The air-cooled unit is based on the old GPz1100 – strong, almost over-engineered, and still a favourite with drag racers and tuners. Freed from the need to produce awesome peak power figures for maximum speed, the engine designers were able to concentrate on getting smooth, strong, useable power from as little as 2,000rpm all the way up to the relatively lowly 9,500rpm red line.

The only concession to the technological advances made since the 'seventies is the air-cooled motor's twin plug set-up. The use of two spark plugs per cylinder helps improve combustion efficiency and beefs up an already fearsome midrange power curve – there are few bikes that give the same impression of arm-tugging acceleration as an 1100 Zephyr. In the real world, the Zephyr's power characteristics make it easy to drive off the line fast, or power hard out of turns without worrying what gear you're in.

If the midrange is impressive, the Zephyr's high speed manners are less so. Flat out at around 140mph, the combination of old-tech chassis and suspension components, and a riding position that turns you into a sail, means the Zephyr weaves and wobbles along seemingly on the very edge of control. Unless you want to lie flat on the tank, 130mph is a more realistic top speed, and the lack of a fairing means anything over 90mph is uncomfortable for long distances.

But paradoxically, it's this very aspect that makes the Zephyr so popular. Not everyone wants a bike that can do 170mph and handles so well you have to be a budding racer to take it to its limits. There's definitely a place for the Zephyr's low tech, low cost, high fun factor approach, as Honda, Suzuki and Yamaha have since proved by following Kawasaki's lead and producing their own contributions to the retro revolution.

SPECIFICATION: KAWASAKI 1100 ZEPHYR	
ENGINE	Air-cooled DOHC 8-valve in-line four
DISPLACEMENT	1062cc
HORSEPOWER	91bhp @ 7900rpm
CARBURETTORS	4 x 34mm Keihin
GEAR BOX	Five speed
FRAME	Tubular steel double cradle
WHEELBASE	59.1in
WEIGHT	534lbs dry
TOP SPEED	140mph

'There are few bikes that give the same impression of arm-tugging acceleration as an 1100 Zephyr.'

Kawasaki ZX-9R

....

'Accelerating effortlessly from a standstill up to an indicated 170mph without pausing for breath.'

Almost as fast as the awesome ZZ-R1100, the ZX-9R packs a ferocious punch into a far more compact package.

Kawasaki have long been known as manufacturers of superlative superbikes. From the days of the Z1, through the 900 Ninja, to the ZZ-R1100, they have built an enviable reputation for building ultimate in-line fours. Rather than expending time and money on innovation for its own sake and technological dead-ends, the Big 'K' has stuck to what it knows, and perfected it. They have taken the water-cooled DOHC 16-valve in-line four and made it their own.

In recent years Kawasaki have concentrated their efforts in the superbike market on large capacity sports-tourers such as the ZZ-R1100, with the ZXR750 presenting the pinnacle of supersports development in their range. But with the advent of Honda's all-conquering Fireblade, Kawasaki had to produce a fire-breathing 900cc race-replica of their own. The ZX-9R is it, although this is a street racer with a difference.

Rather than produce a bike that featured state-of-the-art handling and race-track performance, Kawasaki attempted to bridge the gap between race-replica and sports-tourer, to produce a bike that had the looks and speed of a race-replica, but which was comfortable for two-up road-riding. They reasoned that some motorcyclists want the style and image of a race-replica, but the comfort and practicality of a more traditional road bike.

To achieve this Kawasaki made it just a little bit bigger and heavier than a mere Kawasaki 'Fireblade'. Without the need to save weight wherever possible they could concentrate on building a superbike that looked suitably aggressive but which was big enough and comfortable enough to satisfy the demands of the man in the street.

Lashings of extra mid-range power makes the 9R easier to ride than the ZXR750, yet it is almost as nimble as its smaller stablemate.

But that doesn't mean the ZX-9R isn't a fine sportsbike in its own right. With a water-cooled DOHC 16-valve in-line four cylinder engine pumping out 125bhp, and a lightweight but strong aluminium-alloy beam frame, the ZX-9R is a performance superbike capable of exceeding 165mph. Multi-adjustable inverted telescopic front forks and a rising-rate rear monoshock give the ZX-9R up-to-the-minute suspension technology and ensure that the handling is as impressive as the engine performance.

Weighing in at 475lbs dry the ZX-9R is no lightweight (it's 70lbs heavier than a Honda CBR900 Fireblade), but that doesn't count against it anywhere except on a race track. On the road the ZX-9R is lightning-quick, blessed with masses of mid-range power and a top-end delivery that takes your breath

away. Accelerating effortlessly from a standstill up to an indicated 170mph without pausing for breath, the ZX-9R is the kind of bike that will cover distances quickly, comfortably and with the minimum of fuss. Not quite as quickly and effortlessly as a ZZ-R1100, but not far off, and with the styling and looks of a bike that belongs on a race track.

SPECIFICATION: KAWASAKI ZX-9R	
ENGINE	Water-cooled DOHC 16-valve in-line four
DISPLACEMENT	899cc
HORSEPOWER	125bhp @ 10,500rpm
CARBURETTORS	4 x 40mm Keihin
GEAR BOX	6 speed
FRAME	Aluminium-alloy twin beam
WHEELBASE	56.7ins
WEIGHT	475lbs dry
TOP SPEED	167mph

Kawasaki ZXR750

By 1989 Kawasaki badly needed a sports 750 to challenge Honda's RC30, Suzuki's ever-improving GSX-R and Yamaha's ageing but still potent FZ750. The answer was the ZXR750. Based on the firm's ZX-7, a successful World Endurance contender, the ZXR pitched Kawasaki straight back into the 750-class limelight – both on the track and in the showrooms.

The basic formula was conventional enough – an in-line, four cylinder engine in an alloy twin spar frame with wheels, brakes and tyre sizes calculated to get the ZXR up to speed in the new World Superbike Championships. The bodywork, too, was straight from the factory race bikes, with twin headlights to match the ZXR's 150mph capabilities.

The early models quickly got a reputation for outstanding handling and razor-sharp steering, but at the expense of a racer-firm ride which could be uncomfortable on bumpy roads. The completely revised J1 model of 1991 was a huge improvement, but still had over-stiff rear suspension. 1992 brought a softer rear spring, and the facelift for 1993 finally brought the ZXR's ride quality up to the same standard as its handling and power. Even those who criticised the rear suspension, though, had no complaints about the front. From 1991 onwards the ZXR got class-leading upside-down forks and immensely powerful brakes which take a racetrack to push to their limits. The styling was updated, too, from the early bike's purposeful, slabby look to a more streamlined design, but the riding position remained aggressive – a real racetrack cocktail of low handlebars (for a wind-cheating crouch), high seat and high footpegs (for extra ground clearance).

The engine evolved at the same rate as the chassis. Early models produced competitive power figures, but needed to be revved hard all the time to stay 'on the pipe'. 1991's J model was stronger but, crucially, produced peak torque at lower revs, making the bike much easier to ride on the road. More engine modifications followed in 1993, with

Although one of the least expensive of supersport 750s, the Kawasaki offers an exhilarating combination of raw power and precision handling, not to mention consistent World Superbike honours.

No other road-going 750 is quite so sure-footed into turns as the ZXR, but it took a long time to get the rear suspension sorted.

higher compression and revised valvegear pushing peak power back up the rev range again. What really made it fly, though, was its secret weapon – new air intakes based on the successful ZZ-R1100 system.

From the start, ZXRs had air intakes in the fairing, feeding cool air through hoses above the tank to the airbox. For race use, these could be converted to pressurize the airbox at high speed, giving extra power and allowing the engine to rev higher. Now the road bike got that same advantage. The result was a bike that could hit a genuine 165mph in absolutely standard trim, making it the fastest in its class.

In race form, too, there are few bikes that can match the ZXR's all-round performance. From 24-hour Endurance racing to World Superbikes, the ZXR has won just about everything going, and its conventional layout means even privateers without access to factory parts have a chance of success. Many of the fastest ZXR racers in the world are privately-owned and entered bikes.

But the ZXR's road manners are at the heart of its success. It has always managed to combine its race-track looks with the solid virtues of easy servicing and predictable handling. It has also always managed to be just a little cheaper than its direct competitors.

But that's only half the story. As soon as you thumb the starter and hear the engine growl into life below the tank, you're in a different world – a world of chequered flags and podiums rather than traffic lights and diesel fumes. As the speed rises and the engine growl gives way to the wail of the intake and exhaust, you can kid yourself you're Scott Russell on the Daytona banking, or John Reynolds at Brands Hatch, or Terry Rymer at Le Mans. The real reason the ZXR has found a place in the hearts (and garages) of so many sportsbike riders is simple. A well set-up ZXR is quite simply one of the most exciting road bikes in the world.

'As soon as you thumb the starter and hear the engine growl into life below the tank, you're in a different world.'

SPECIFICATION: KAWASAKI ZXR750	
ENGINE	Water-cooled DOHC 16-valve in-line four
DISPLACEMENT	749cc
HORSEPOWER	120bhp @ 11,000rpm
CARBURETTORS	4 x 36mm Keihin
GEAR BOX	Six speed
FRAME	Aluminium twin spar
WHEELBASE	56.3ins
WEIGHT	452lbs dry
TOP SPEED	165mph

Kawasaki ZZ-R1100

·····················

The Kawasaki ZZ-R1100 is one of the ultimates in the superbikes world. Hugely powerful, stunningly fast and very sleek, the ZZ-R1100 brings eye-watering performance to the mass-market.

Capable of out-performing just about any car on the roads (even the like of Ferarris and Porsches), the ZZ-R1100 costs less than the price of a family saloon. With a top-speed nudging 180mph and a 0-60mph time of less than three seconds, the ZZ-R1100 is a true king of the roads.

So what is surprising about the ZZ-R1100 is how ordinary it really is. It doesn't rely on complicated suspension systems, fancy fuel-injection or curiously-shaped pistons. No, the ZZ-R1100 uses solid, well-proven engine technology and state-of-the-art aerodynamics to produce one of the most impressive superbikes ever seen.

The heart of the ZZ-R1100 is its water-cooled, double overhead cam, 16-valve, in-line four-cylinder engine. Power output varies from country to country according to local laws, but in unrestricted form the ZZ-R1100 makes a whopping 147bhp at 11,000rpm. With a dry weight of 514lbs, that gives the ZZ-R1100 a power-to-weight ratio five times higher than a *very* fast car. One hundred and eighty miles per hour and a standing quarter of a mile in under 11 seconds is territory normally reserved for Italian supercars, but the ZZ-R1100 makes it available to the man in the street!

And what of the rest of the ZZ-R1100? The svelte bodywork is a major contributor to the awesome top speed and it also helps to keep the wind and rain away from the rider. Suspension is handled by a hefty pair of 43mm multi-adjustable telescopic forks at the front and a rising-rate, multi-adjustable monoshock at the back. Twin 320mm front discs seized by four-piston calipers give the ZZ-R much-needed stopping power, with a single 250mm rear disc gripped by a twin-piston caliper to complete the set-up.

The ZZ-R1100 isn't a pure sportsbike, nor was it ever intended to be. Kawasaki have eschewed the race-replica route for their litre bikes, preferring instead to make them potent all-rounders. As a

More 'super' than most, the ZZ-R1100 is the fastest production motorcycle ever built, capable of humbling cars costing ten times the price.

Although not so nimble as Honda's Fireblade, the big 'Kwacker' scratches better than anything *this* big has a right to do.

'The ZZ-R1100 brings eye-watering performance to the mass-market.'

result the ZZ-R1100 is an excellent two-up sports-tourer capable of covering long distances quickly and easily. A large fuel tank and reasonably frugal consumption make the ZZ-R a good long-distance machine, and the rider and pillion accommodation are appropriately comfortable.

There aren't many superbikes with the all-round capabilities of the ZZ-R1100. On the one hand it is a fast, sure-footed sportsbike capable of deliver-ing exceptional performance at the twist of the wrist, while on the other hand it will carry two people a long way in reasonable comfort and with the minimum of fuss. Small wonder, then, that Kawasaki sell so many of them.

Whether it's tricks you want (left), or 1000 touring miles in a day, the ZZ-R1100 effortlessly delivers.

SPECIFICATION: KAWASAKI ZZ-R1100	
ENGINE	Liquid-cooled DOHC 16-valve in-line four
DISPLACEMENT	1052cc
HORSEPOWER	147bhp @ 11000rpm
CARBURETTORS	4 x 40mm Keihin CV
GEAR BOX	Six speed
FRAME	Aluminium-alloy twin beam
WHEELBASE	58.8ins
WEIGHT	514lbs dry
TOP SPEED	175mph

Magni Australia

························

'It was on a twisty road, though, that the Australia came into its own.'

A red-and-silver tribute to countless MV *Grand Prix* winners, but the transverse V-twin is every inch a Moto Guzzi — with added Magni class.

Its sleek styling, big V-twin engine and enormous rear tyre showed that this was a serious sports bike, but it was the red-and-silver paintwork that revealed most about the Magni Australia. Those were the colours of the legendary MV Agusta race team once run by Arturo Magni, the Australia's creator.

Magni had prepared the 'Gallarate Fire Engines' raced to glory by John Surtees, Mike Hailwood and Giacomo Agostini. Then, when MV stopped racing after winning 17 consecutive 500cc world titles between 1958 and 1974, Magni set up business with his son Giovanni to build high-quality roadsters from a workshop near Agusta's old base at Gallarate, north of Milan. Several used engines from Moto Guzzi, notably the 1990-model Sfida, a

retro-styled sportster powered by the two-valves-per-cylinder engine from the Le Mans.

Two years later came the fastest and best Magni yet: the Australia, so-called because it was a direct descendent of a Guzzi-engined Magni racebike that had notched up a string of impressive results Down Under. The Australia was powered by the V-twin engine from the Daytona 1000, Guzzi's fuel-injected, eight-valve flagship. To ease homologation the 992cc 'high cam' unit was retained in its entirety from airbox to silencers.

Almost everything else was new, though, most notably the frame. In place of the Daytona's large-diameter spine was a more conventional arrangement, based on three 34mm diameter chrome-molybdenum steel tubes running back

Unlike more commonplace Guzzis, the Australia's steering is light and precise, a tribute to the exceptional quality of its chassis and suspension.

from the steering head. A pair of front downtubes helped secure the engine.

The swing-arm was a single-shock version of Magni's proven Parallelogramo design, created to combat torque-reaction. Rear suspension was provided by a single shock from Dutch firm White Power. The Australia's swing-arm was wide enough to allow fitment of a wide, 180-section rear tyre.

At the front were upside-down Forcelle Italia forks – adjustable, like the shock, for both compression and rebound damping. The 17-inch wheels held 320mm Brembo brake discs with four-piston calipers. Both mudguards were lightweight carbon fibre, helping to keep weight to a respectable 450lb dry.

The cylinder heads visible at each side of the Australia made the Guzzi connection clear, and there was no doubting the engine's origins when it fired up to send the bike rocking in characteristic fashion with every blip of the throttle. At most engine speeds the Australia had a wonderfully loose, rev-happy feel, aided by the Weber-Marelli fuel-injection's crisp response.

With a peak output of 95bhp, the slippery Australia had a top speed of about 140mph, plus generous acceleration from low revs. The Magni pulled strongly almost from tickover, with a slight surge at around 4000rpm that sent it charging along

with a rustling from the aircooled engine's sticking-out cylinders, and a typically long-legged Guzzi feel at high speed.

It was on a twisty road, though, that the Australia came into its own. Its Brembo brakes were superbly powerful, steering was light and the Magni could be cornered easily and with great precision. Suspension was compliant but very well-controlled at both ends, and the drive shaft barely noticeable.

That blend of good looks, effortless engine performance and nimble handling made the Australia a very impressive special, with a captivating blend of pace and grace. Its price was high – but not excessively so for a machine hand-built in tiny numbers. Especially when those hands had once built bikes for legends such as Surtees, Hailwood and Agostini.

Fuel injection helps give the big Guzzi motor impressive responsiveness and punch throughout the rev range, with an un-Guzzi-like eagerness to rev.

SPECIFICATION: MAGNI AUSTRALIA	
ENGINE	Air-cooled high-cam 8-valve 90-degree transverse V-twin
DISPLACEMENT	992cc
HORSEPOWER	95bhp
CARBURETTORS	Weber-Marelli fuel-injection
GEAR BOX	Five speed
FRAME	Tubular steel
WHEELBASE	58ins
WEIGHT	450lbs dry
TOP SPEED	140mph

Moto Guzzi Daytona 1000

'The Daytona 1000 is a true Moto Guzzi in that it is long, low and stable.'

In the mid-1970s Moto Guzzis were exotic Italian superbikes par excellence. The Le Mans was considered one of the finest superbikes on the road, and although the price was considerably higher than the Japanese equivalent, there was no shortage of customers for these Italian thoroughbreds.

But time and technological innovation wait for no one, and they certainly didn't wait for Moto Guzzi who were content to rest on their laurels rather than try to compete with the increasingly innovative Japanese manufacturers. By the mid-1980s Moto Guzzi were still expensive compared to Oriental competitors, but they were no longer a match for the modern Japanese superbike. The slow-revving push-rod four-valve twins could no longer compete on equal terms with the new generation of high-revving DOHC 16-valve fours.

But by the early 1990s the Italians were back on top, or at least competing with the Japanese on equal terms for performance and price. And Moto Guzzi's contribution to the renaissance of the Italian motorcycle industry was the Daytona 1000. For several years Moto Guzzi were rumoured to have a new

four-valve 1000cc V-twin superbike ready to go into production, and it finally appeared on the streets in 1993.

The Daytona 1000 is a true Moto Guzzi in that it is long, low and stable, yet it has a very modern and powerful engine. The 1000cc V-twin motor has four valves per cylinder and is fuel-injected, giving it an output of 95bhp at 8000rpm and producing a healthy 72lb/ft of torque at 6000rpm. Okay, so that's not going to give GSX-R1100 owners too many sleepless nights, but for a Moto Guzzi that's pretty impressive and is capable of taking the Daytona 1000 to a genuine top speed of 145mph – not bad for an air-cooled twin.

Interestingly, the 1000 Daytona still has the traditional Moto Guzzi shaft drive, which is unusual for a sportsbike. But Moto Guzzi also employed a clever parallelogram rear swingarm arrangement to counteract the shaft's torque effect. With a multi-adjustable Koni monoshock at the rear (compressed

Imposing Daytona lines follow in the noble tradition of 25 years of Guzzi big twins.

Long, slow steering and stable — the latest Guzzi (left) spurns Fireblade-style handling in favour of more relaxed real-world virtues.

To the familiar Guzzi transverse Vee (below), the Daytona adds four-valve heads and state-of-the-art fuel injection.

by cantilever linkage rather than a rising-rate arrangement), and a pair of Marzocchi telescopic front forks with rebound damping adjustment, the handling of the Daytona is sure-footed if rather ponderous compared to the latest-generation superbikes from Japan.

Riding the Daytona is a curious experience. It's incredibly fast for a Moto Guzzi, it handles surprisingly well for a Moto Guzzi and yet compared to most modern superbikes it still feels quaintly old-fashioned, an endearing mixture of old and new.

But it is the styling and traditional feel, combined with modern performance and handling, that makes the Daytona such an exceptional machine. When everyone thought that Moto Guzzi had had their day, they managed to produce a bike that was both beautiful, stylish, totally individual, and yet which retained all that was special and desirable about the marque.

SPECIFICATION: MOTO GUZZI DAYTONA 1000	
ENGINE	Air-cooled SOHC 8-valve V-twin
DISPLACEMENT	992cc
HORSEPOWER	95bhp @ 8000rpm
CARBURETTORS	Electronic fuel injection
GEAR BOX	5 speed
FRAME	Tubular steel spine
WHEELBASE	58.3ins
WEIGHT	474lbs dry
TOP SPEED	145mph

Moto Guzzi 1100 Sport

Big, simple, handsome and strong, the 1100 Sport was a mid-'90s sports bike of the old school. The latest in a long line of Moto Guzzi V-twins to be fitted with the Italian firm's traditional pushrod-operated transverse V-twin engine, the Sport was introduced in 1994 as a cheaper version of the eight-valve Daytona 1000. The new bike dispensed with the Daytona's costly fuel-injection system in favour of a simple pair of 40mm Dell'Orto carburettors, as used by Guzzi for decades. If the result was inevitably a little crude by contemporary standards, the Sport still made for a rapid and charismatic roadburner.

Its engine was essentially that of the faithful two-valves-per-cylinder Le Mans sportster, with bore and stroke increased to give a capacity of 1064cc. The Sport's larger pistons also gave a reshaped combustion chamber. Other changes including revised camshaft design and a lighter crankshaft combined to produce Guzzi's most powerful two-

Classic Guzzi lines make an appealing change from lookalike oriental race replicas. Guzzi retain the same unshakable faith in the transverse V-twin engine layout which has served them well for over 25 years.

valve motor yet, its claimed peak output of 90bhp being 5bhp lower than the Daytona's figure.

This new engine sat in a steel spine frame closely related to that of the Daytona, and used a similar suspension combination of 41mm Marzocchi forks and remote-reservoir rear shock from Dutch specialists White Power. Wheel sizes remained 17 inch front and 18 rear, the Sport's only cycle-part change being that its four-piston Brembo front brake calipers gripped larger, 320mm discs. The Sport's subtle restyle incorporated a new seat unit that made room for an occasional pillion while maintaining a lean and purposeful look.

The bike felt every bit a Moto Guzzi as its V-twin motor churned into life with a characteristic lurch from its longitudinal crankshaft. The aggressive riding position pulled the pilot forward to the low handlebars, with seat and footrests set high, and was ill suited to town use – as was the Sport's rather clunky transmission and hesitant power

The 1100 Sport is in its element thundering along fast highways like this in the Italian Lakes. On mountain hairpins it becomes more unwieldy.

delivery below 3000rpm. Once spinning properly, though, the big V-twin thudded along with even more of the characteristic torque and charm that have traditionally made Guzzis so enjoyable.

The V-twin unit's strong midrange performance encouraged short-shifting through the slow but fairly precise gearbox, and meant there was little need to take the tacho needle to the 8000rpm redline. The typical low-pitched V-twin vibration never became unpleasant, and the Sport felt unstressed as it cruised at 100mph with just 5000rpm showing on its tachometer. Revved harder, the Sport's lightened engine internals helped it accelerate with very respectable enthusiasm towards a top speed of 140mph.

Handling was typical of a Guzzi, combining slow but neutral steering, firm suspension and excellent high-speed stability. The Sport was not best suited to slow, twisty roads, feeling rather long and unwieldy. But once into a turn the bike felt reassuringly precise, and it thundered through faster curves with ease. On smooth surfaces, in particular, its stability, ground-clearance and the grip of its Michelin Hi-Sport radial tyres made the Sport a

genuinely quick superbike. Braking power was good, too, thanks to the uprated Brembo set-up, although this was not fitted with Guzzi's traditional linked system.

The 1100 Sport lacked the power and handling finesse of more sophisticated sports bike opposition, and it couldn't match the impact of earlier Guzzi chargers such as the legendary Le Mans Mk.1 of 1975. But the Sport was stylish, competitively priced and succeeded in delivering stirring performance in a typically relaxed manner. Most of all, it proved there was still plenty of life in Guzzi's familiar transverse V-twin format.

SPECIFICATION: MOTO GUZZI 1100 SPORT	
ENGINE	Air-cooled OHV 4-valve transverse 90-degree V-twin
DISPLACEMENT	1062cc
HORSEPOWER	90bhp @ 7500rpm
CARBURETTORS	2 x 40mm Dell'Orto
GEAR BOX	Five speed
FRAME	Tubular steel spine
WHEELBASE	58.3ins
WEIGHT	440lbs dry
TOP SPEED	140mph

No fuel injection, and a mere two valves per cylinder, but the Sport packs a deceptive mid-range punch that few Japanese multis can match.

Suzuki GSX-R750

·······················

'What it lacks in pure top speed it makes up for in agility.'

The Suzuki GSX-R750 is one of the most successful superbikes ever made. Successful not only as a top-selling bike around the world, but also as one of the all-time great racing motorcycles. It is believed that more races have been won aboard GSX-R750s than any other motorcycle. For a bike that has been in production for only a decade that's quite an achievement – but what a decade!

The GSX-R750 was launched back in 1985 and was at the forefront of the race-replica boom that followed. Everyone wanted a bike that looked as though it had just come off the starting grid of a *Grand Prix*, and the GSX-R750 was exactly that. The twin-headlamp fairing, sporting riding position and exceptional performance offered by its four-cylinder 750cc engine made it an instant hit.

At its launch the GSX-R's engine was unusual in that it was oil- rather than water-cooled. The rest

of the GSX-R's engine was standard stuff for the period – a double overhead camshaft, four valves-per-cylinder, across-the-frame in-line four – but built exceedingly light. Its power was also exceptional; almost 100bhp from a road-going 750 was unheard of.

A decade later the GSX-R750 is still an uncompromising race-replica, although it has undergone a few fundamental changes. In its latest incarnation the GSX-R is now a water-cooled across-the-frame in-line four putting out 117bhp. The designers at Suzuki have spent much time and even more money perfecting and refining the GSX-R750, and although it may not be winning as many races as it used to, it is still one of the top-selling superbikes around the world.

And with good reason. The engine is powerful and smooth, giving the GSX-R eye-watering performance and a top speed of around 155mph. It

Ten years ago the first GSX-R invented the rev-crazy race-replica concept, and remains the concept by which other sports 750s are judged.

is still the high-revving, race-track oriented bike it always was, reacting better to the harsh treatment usually meted out by motorcycle racers than to the gentle touch. The GSX-R is a bike that likes to be ridden hard, and when it is it performs superbly.

What it lacks in pure top speed it makes up for in agility. The aluminium-alloy double-cradle chassis and state-of-the-art suspension front and rear give the GSX-R almost peerless handling, and twin front disc brakes and a single rear disc make it one of the fastest-stopping bikes around. With a dry weight of 458lbs the GSX-R is not the lightweight it once was, but much of that weight goes unnoticed when the throttle is cracked open and the horizon comes hurtling towards you.

The GSX-R has always been sleek and good looking, and although the transition to water

cooling has piled on the pounds in recent years it is still a handsome beast that conjures up an impression of speed and excitement even when parked. And it is those aggressive, no-nonsense good looks that are part of the GSX-R's appeal.

Although an uncom-promising beast (this bike was not built for commuting or two-up touring), the GSX-R750 is more exciting and fulfilling to ride than many other faster machines simply due to the fact that it demands excellence from the rider before it will deliver its full superbike performance.

Multi-adjustable suspension at both ends allows the GSX-R to be fine-tuned to meet most road conditions.

SPECIFICATION: SUZUKI GSX-R750	
ENGINE	Liquid-cooled DOHC 16-valve in-line four
DISPLACEMENT	749cc
HORSEPOWER	117bhp @ 11500rpm
CARBURETTORS	Four 38mm Mikuni
GEARBOX	Six speed
FRAME	Aluminium-alloy double-cradle
WHEELBASE	56.5ins
WEIGHT	458lbs dry
TOP SPEED	155mph

Suzuki GSX-R1100

·······················

When it comes to ultimate superbikes, they don't come much more ultimate than this. Suzuki's GSX-R1100 is one of the biggest, most powerful, and awe-inspiring superbikes ever built.

Unveiled back in 1986 to enormous acclaim, the GSX-R1100 (like its pioneering smaller sibling, the GSX-R750) has undergone many changes over the ensuing years. At its launch the big GSX-R was light, very powerful and wickedly fast. And over the years the Suzuki, pressurised by competition – primarily from Yamaha's FZR1000 – piled on more

Suzuki's big bruiser isn't jet-propelled – quite. But a handful of the 1100's throttle at 9000rpm is as close to supersonic as most riders are ever likely to get.

and more power. But the trade-off was more and more weight gained, and by the early 1990s the GSX-R1100 had become a muscle-bound monster. Putting out 145bhp in stock (but unrestricted) trim the GSX-R scaled over 500lbs fuelled up. That's a lot of bike producing a lot of power.

But now the GSX-R1100 has undergone another transformation and although it is still big, heavy and fast, it is no longer the bad mannered behemoth it once was. Gone is the wayward handling and peculiar steering, replaced by an altogether more docile beast.

What happened was that Suzuki radically updated the GSX-R1100's motor, turning it from an oil-cooled to a water-cooled affair. They did the same thing to the GSX-R750 in 1992 and the result was a bike that was better than ever, but not by much. The main reason for adopting water-cooling is not that it's more efficient, but because it's quieter – an important consideration in these days of increasingly stringent noise regulations.

In its latest incarnation the GSX-R1100 is much improved. The water-cooling adds weight, but the engine has been otherwise revised to make it lighter overall, partly through the use of exotic magnesium engine parts. Having said that, the GSX-R1100 still tips the scales at 485lbs dry – considerably more than bikes like the Fireblade or FZR1000 EXUP, but less than it used to.

The aluminium-alloy cradle frame has also been revised for increased rigidity, and up front a pair of 43mm multi-adjustable inverted telescopic forks make the handling and steering more stable and sure-footed than before. At the back a rising-rate multi-adjustable monoshock helps put all that power to the road whilst keeping things nice and smooth.

On the road the GSX-R is fearsomely fast. With a power output of 145bhp in unrestricted form, the GSX-R will rocket up to 175mph in very short order and can turn in standing-quarter times in under 11 seconds (and 0-60mph in under three seconds) if you can keep the front wheel on the ground and prevent the rear tyre spinning excessively. It still feels like a big, heavy sportsbike and lacks the finesse of Honda's and Yamaha's finest sports machinery, but for going frighteningly fast between corners not many motorcycles can touch it.

'By the early 1990s the GSX-R1100 had become a muscle-bound monster.'

SPECIFICATION: SUZUKI GSX-R1100

ENGINE	Water-cooled DOHC 16-valve in-line four
DISPLACEMENT	1074cc
HORSEPOWER	145bhp @ 10,000rpm
CARBURETTORS	4 x 38mm Keihin
GEAR BOX	5 speed
FRAME	Aluminium-alloy twin cradle
WHEELBASE	55.5ins
WEIGHT	485lbs dry
TOP SPEED	175mph

Suzuki RF900

....

'Suzuki saw the gap for a slightly softer-edged machine.'

When Honda's Fireblade rekindled interest in the 900 class in 1992, the other manufacturers were caught on the hop. For Suzuki the matter was urgent – overnight the Fireblade had usurped both the GSX-R1100's position as the definitive nutter's bike, and the GSX-R750's top spot in the handling stakes. But it had also gained a reputation as a bike which was hard to get the best out of – a real racer on the road. Suzuki saw the gap for a slightly softer-edged machine, easier to use and more practical, but still possessing awesome straight-line performance. The RF900 – styled and badged as a big brother to the existing RF600 – was launched for 1994.

Like the RF600, the 900 was built to a tight budget, developing existing technology rather than starting from scratch with a whole new design.

The water-cooled engine is based on the well-proven GSX-R range, and combines the free-revving nature of the 750 with the low-down pulling power of the 1100. But it's far more than just a sleeved-down 1100 or a big-bore 750. The RF's engine is so well-developed it has a character all of its own. The carburation, in particular, is perfect, allowing the rider to crack the throttle open at any revs and be rewarded with instant performance. Whilst the 900's outright performance doesn't set any records – slightly faster in still conditions than a Fireblade but a long way off the class-leading 170mph+ of the ZX-9, its real strength is in its all-round performance.

The surprise package of '94, Suzuki's RF900 exploded onto the scene with blistering performance at a truly amazing bargain price.

The RF's styling, inherited from its RF600 stablemate, isn't to everyone's taste. But as in so many other areas, the RF's policy of getting the job done first and worrying about appearances later pays off. The fairing does an excellent job of directing air around the rider, and the bulbous tail unit carries a seriously wide and comfortable seat with a proper pillion grab rail. The RF is one of the few serious performance bikes that are genuinely comfortable two-up.

Despite pushing it very close in the performance stakes, the steel-framed RF was never meant to compete head-on with the Fireblade, and weighs in around 40lbs heavier than Honda's rocketship. In theory that puts the Suzuki at a serious disadvantage, but in the real world the extra weight gives the RF a comfortable ride, with a feeling of solidity that the pared-down 'Blade can't achieve. It does this with old-tech, but well-matched, suspension components – no fashionable upside-down forks or single-sided swingarms here. But that doesn't mean the RF can't corner hard – it can. The weight distribution's more sporty than touring, and the emphasis is on stability. 120mph sweeping bends are the RF900's favourite stamping grounds, but it tackles everything from backroads to the occasional racetrack with the same easy, do-anything, go-anywhere competence.

For anyone trying an RF900 for the first time, there are two surprises. First, that something apparently styled for long-distance comfort offers such shattering performance and competent, hard-charging handling. Second, that it's cheap – nearly ten per cent cheaper than Suzuki's own GSX-R750. If the Fireblade broke the mould by proving that big bikes didn't need to be bruising heavyweights, the RF did the same by proving that high performance need not cost the Earth.

The RF's prodigious horsepower gleefully shrugs off the limitations of a heavy steel frame and slightly down-market suspension.

SPECIFICATION: SUZUKI RF900	
ENGINE	Water-cooled DOHC 16-valve in-line four
DISPLACEMENT	937cc
HORSEPOWER	124bhp @ 10,000rpm
CARBURETTORS	4 x 36mm Mikuni
GEAR BOX	Six speed
FRAME	Pressed steel twin spar
WHEELBASE	56.7ins
WEIGHT	447lbs dry
TOP SPEED	165mph

Comparatively restrained styling reflects the 900's role as a high-speed all-rounder rather than a race track escapee.

Triumph Daytona 900

'There are no bottom-end flat spots, just a rising tide of willing revs.'

Almost overnight, this Superbike became a classic. When the new Triumph range was unveiled in 1991, it comprised four engines: triples of 750 and 900cc, and 1000cc and 1200cc fours. The 750cc engine is now confined to just one model, the 1200 to two, whilst the 1000 has disappeared altogether. There is a very good reason for this: the 900cc triple has fast earned a reputation as one of motorcycling's great powerplants. As well as the Daytona, the same basic engine powers the Thunderbird, Trident, Sprint, Tiger, Trophy, Speed Triple and Super III.

Of these, the Daytona models are the most sporting. The Super III is a tuned and slightly lightened version of the Daytona which offers little more, other than a hefty price tag and better brakes.

Although notionally a sports machine, the Daytona is not in the same mould as Japanese race replicas such as Suzuki's GSX-Rs, compared to which it feels long, tall and heavy. It cannot flick through chicanes like a GP machine, and it doesn't rev way into five figures. But the Daytona is deceptive. Its point-to-point performance is superb.

Most of the credit for this belongs to *that* engine. Compared to the awesome power of the four-cylinder 1200 Daytona, the three is a better balanced and more enticing machine. It ticks over with a slightly cantankerous rumble which, balance shafts or no balance shafts, says 'I'm an engine' rather than merely a sealed box full of motive effort. From the instant you press the button, Triumph triples exude the sort of character that Japan largely designed out years ago.

There are no bottom-end flat spots, just a rising tide of willing revs. Like a four, the Daytona is content to potter from sub-tickover speeds; useful power begins to swell at 3000rpm, continuing unabated until the 9500rpm red line. And at no point does it ever feel remotely stressed.

SPECIFICATION: TRIUMPH DAYTONA 900	
ENGINE	Liquid-cooled DOHC 16-valve transverse four
DISPLACEMENT	885cc
HORSEPOWER	100bhp @ 9500rpm
CARBURETTORS	3 x 36mm Mikuni CV
GEAR BOX	Six speed
FRAME	Tubular steel spine
WHEELBASE	58.7ins
WEIGHT	476lbs dry
TOP SPEED	148mph

Bold styling, superb finish and a lusty engine made the Daytona triple an instant hit when first introduced in 1993. Most testers rate it the best balanced of the Daytona range.

Although not so fast as Japanese 900s, the Daytona's bottomless power brings effortless performance with minimal use of the gears.

'Daytona' might be American, but the Union flag marks the 900 as British — and proud of it.

Peak revs equates to 148mph in top gear, which might not seem impressive in an age of 150mph 600s. But it is the manner of the triple's getting there that sets it apart. There's no need to reconcile road speed to two decimal places of revs: just wind it on, and watch it disappear. Whilst most engines of comparable flexibility are either bland or plain slow, the 900 is an unburstably quick projectile from A to B.

The rest of the package is of the same high quality. The gearchange is positive, with no under-selection, the truck-sized clutch practically redundant once on the move. Six speeds is overkill, but allows relaxed top gear ratios. In almost every area, the engines are over-engineered (regularly doing 100 hours at well over 11,000 full-throttle rpm on the test bench), with elaborate attention to oil-tightness.

Due to its sheer weight and lazy steering geometry (27°/105mm), the Daytona is never going to rival the FZR Yamaha, much less Honda's Fireblade, for rapid flicks through tight corners. It is, like the ZZ-R, more of a hyper sports-tourer than an out-and-out sports machine.

Charging through ultra-fast sweepers, steering and stability is second to none. Even on standard settings, damping is good, with no trace of wallow. The converse – betraying the same conservatism as went into the engine – is a lack of flickability through tight stuff. It's a reassuring formula which responds better the faster the road. For above all, the 900 loves going quickly, thrives on being thrashed. It's a Superbike that begs to be ridden. And *hard*.

Triumph Daytona 1200

······························

When the re-born Triumph factory emerged on the world stage in 1991, it established its credentials with a pair of touring bikes – the Trophy 1200 and 900 – and a pair of basic, unfaired triples – the Trident 750 and 900.

But it soon became clear that there was a section of the market ready to be offered an alternative to big Japanese superbikes. Triumph's answer was the Daytona 1200, introduced in 1993.

Under the skin, it's much the same as the rest of the Triumph range – same frame, same geometry, same engine. The main difference is the firmer suspension and sports compound tyres, giving a completely different, tauter feel than the Daytona's Trophy stablemate. Swoopy, aerodynamic body-work in eyecatching colours reinforces the image of a bike built for speed.

The 1180cc engine is based on the Trophy 1200's proven unit. But while the Trophy makes do with 106bhp, sportier cams and some revised cylinder head dimensions help take the Daytona to a claimed 147bhp at the crankshaft, making it one of the most powerful standard motorcycle engines in Creation.

But while Kawasaki's ZZ-R1100, Yamaha's FZR1000 and Suzuki's GSX-R1100 fight it out for the title of Fastest Production Bike, the Daytona takes a different approach. Despite its enormous power output, it is geared for a top speed of 'only' 160mph, making for better acceleration at normal road speeds – the Daytona easily outdrags a ZZ-R1100 from 40-100mph. The engine has a solid, unburstable feel, with none of the buzzy, revvy nature of its Japanese competitors – you really feel as if the engine is happy to sit flat out all day long.

And so is the rider. The Daytona's riding position feels almost old-fashioned – upright, with quite high handlebars and low footrests. The fairing, too, keeps most of the wind blast off the rider, making high speed work less of a chore. And that makes the Daytona far more comfortable than just about any other sports bike – and most tourers, too! Long, fast motorway trips on the Daytona

SPECIFICATION: TRIUMPH DAYTONA 1200	
ENGINE	Water-cooled DOHC 16-valve in-line four
DISPLACEMENT	1180cc
HORSEPOWER	147bhp @ 9500rpm
CARBURETTORS	4 x 36mm Mikuni
GEAR BOX	Six speed
FRAME	Steel spine
WHEELBASE	58.7ins
WEIGHT	502lbs dry
TOP SPEED	160mph

On the day of its launch, the British minister of transport criticised the Triumph's performance as 'excessive'. Riders of the awesome 1200 have had far less cause for complaint.

come and go without the aches and pains associated with many big sportsbikes.

But motorways are only half the story. The Daytona is most at home on fast, sweeping A-roads, where its combination of unflappable stability and awesome roll-on power make for fast journey times without the need for constant gear-changing.

On twistier roads, the Daytona's stiffer suspension copes with fast direction changes so easily it's hard to believe it's even related to the

touring Trophy, let alone almost identical. The tyres help too, offering effortless steering and huge amounts of grip – enough to use up even the Daytona's improved ground clearance and strike sparks from the footrests and exhausts in fast turns. Hauling 502lbs of speeding motorcycle to a halt should be hard work, but the Daytona's huge discs and powerful calipers do the job with no fuss at all. It's no race bike – there are plenty of smaller bikes that turn faster and brake harder – what makes the Daytona special is how easy it makes it for the rider to use all it's got to offer. Although theoretically the Triumph is at a weight and handling disadvantage compared to its competitors, it would take a skilled (and brave) ZZ-R or FZR rider to exploit that disadvantage on the road.

It's powerful without being intimidating, and heavy without being cumbersome. It manages to combine the roles of easy-to-ride tourer and blindingly fast sports bike – a neat trick if you can do it. Neat enough to call 'superbike'.

By a long way Britain's fastest-ever production motorcycle, more than any other model the 1200 Daytona established the engineering credentials of the re-born Triumph concern.

'You really feel as if the engine is happy to sit flat out all day long.'

Triumph 900 Speed Triple

'If the good guys ride into town on white Hondas, the bad guys come in on black Speed Triples.'

Other colours are available, but only black really sums up the dark menace of Mr Bloor's audacious baby.

When Triumph rejoined the motorcycle manufacturing fray in the early 1990s the two-wheeled world was impressed. An old and revered name had been applied to a thoroughly modern range of motorcycles and was being sold at prices that allowed Triumphs to compete directly with the Japanese factories.

A few years down the line Triumph have expanded and revised their range, dropping models that didn't sell well and introducing new ones they hoped would. The Speed Triple is one such machine, one which has been received with open arms by the motorcycling fraternity.

Whilst some manufacturers have gone all-out at the retro market, aiming traditional looking machines at the born-again biker, Triumph have taken a different approach. With the Speed Triple they have taken an existing superbike from their range, the Daytona 900, taken off the fairing, and tidied up what is underneath to the point where it is aesthetically pleasing (not an easy thing to do with a modern water-cooled motorcycle). The result is one of the leanest, meanest looking bikes around – a café-racer for the '90s, not a lash-up of bits and pieces designed to look like something from the mid-1970s.

The engine of the Speed Triple is the same excellent unit that powers a whole variety of Triumphs, from the Trophy 900 to the Daytona 900. It is a water-cooled DOHC 12-valve in-line three-cylinder engine that puts out 98bhp and 60lb/ft of torque – enough to dispense with one of the usual six gear ratios. Not massive numbers for a 900, but sufficient to give the Speed Triple a top speed of 140mph.

But outright top speed on an unfaired motorcycle is less important than the speed and ease with which it gets up into three-figure territory. Blessed with plenty of usable torque the Speed Triple lopes along effortlessly at legal speeds, and a quick twist of the throttle will have it careering towards the horizon very quickly.

The chassis, like on all modern Triumphs, is a low-tech, but reasonably capable, tubular steel spine frame using the engine as a stressed-member. Suspension is handled by a pair of adjustable 43mm telescopic forks at the front and a rising-rate multi-adjustable monoshock at the rear. And if the suspension is standard '90s stuff, so are the brakes. With twin 310mm front discs squeezed by Nissin four-piston calipers at the front and a 255mm disc

at the back with a two-piston caliper, the 460lbs Speed Triple can be stopped very quickly and safely.

Out on the open road the Speed Triple is a delight to ride. The smooth, powerful motor keeps the bike moving at an impressive rate, the brakes are superb, and the handling generally good. This isn't the kind of bike to out-handle a state-of-the-art race-replica, but it will acquit itself well in any other company. The huge tyres (a 120/70 x 17 front and massive 180/55 x 17 at the rear) give plenty of grip, and the high, rear-set footrests give generous ground clearance.

But perhaps the most striking thing about the Speed Triple is its sleek good looks. In its black livery, with black painted engine, black exhausts, black wheels and even a black swingarm, the Triumph looks mean and purposeful. There aren't many superbikes around that exude the kind of brutish menace generated by the Speed Triple. If the good guys ride into town on white Hondas, the bad guys come in on black Speed Triples. With the Triple, black truly is beautiful.

Triumph's urban guerrilla is equally at home knifing along country lanes.

(Left) In Speed Triple guise, Hinckley's superbly tractable three proves that five gears are plenty.

SPECIFICATION: TRIUMPH 900 SPEED TRIPLE	
ENGINE	Water-cooled DOHC 12-valve triple
DISPLACEMENT	885cc
HORSEPOWER	98bhp @ 9500rpm
CARBURETTORS	3 x 34mm Mikuni
GEAR BOX	5 speed
FRAME	Tubular-steel spine
WHEELBASE	58.7ins
WEIGHT	460lbs dry
TOP SPEED	140mph

Triumph Sprint 900

....

'The quality of paint and plating is as high as anything in motorcycling.'

The 900 Sprint, like the rest of the Triumph range, is part Superbike, part miracle. After the once-mighty British motorcycle industry self-destructed during the '60s and '70s, the prospects of regeneration on anything like its former scale were as likely as an (old-style) Triumph twin that didn't vibrate or leak oil. True, there had been occasional flourishes from the likes of Norton and Matchless, but these were very small scale and, it turned out, ill-fated.

Triumph is different. To date John Bloor, the Midlands builder who owns the new company, has sunk around £80 million into the venture. The Hinckley, Leicestershire factory is as modern and efficient as any in the world. Its state-of-the-art computer-controlled machinery will produce well over 10,000 motorcycles during 1995. And, most important of all, the product is good.

The Sprint is a case in point. It eschews race replica performance, in favour of a formula which simply works. Yet originally it wasn't even Triumph's idea. When the naked Trident range first appeared in 1991, a number of customisers, notably in Britain and Germany, produced a half-faired variant. One year later Triumph themselves responded with the Sprint.

But there was a difference. Where the 'unofficial' Sprints had simply been modified Tridents, the official version was actually more of a defrocked version of the fully-faired Trophy. So from the outset the Sprint had the Trophy's dual-rate front springs and both pre-load and rebound damping adjustment at the rear. Although still too softly sprung for out-and-out sport riding, the latter is a useful bonus, allowing the suspension to be fine-tuned to suit conditions. On maximum damping, there is less of the mild wallow to which the unfaired bike is prone.

The result not only *looks* like a motorcycle ought, but makes for a versatile and practical all-rounder. Highish 'bars and lower seat offer a riding position as relaxed as anything this side of a full-blown tourer (and better then several of those). Once you've become used to wielding the wide 'bars from low behind the bulbous tank, the bike is beguilingly easy to control. The half fairing largely eliminates wind fatigue. For long trips by motorway or fast A-roads, it is almost indispensable.

SPECIFICATION: TRIUMPH SPRINT 900	
ENGINE	Liquid-cooled DOHC 16-valve transverse four
DISPLACEMENT	885cc
HORSEPOWER	100bhp @ 9500rpm
CARBURETTORS	3 x 36mm Mikuni CV
GEAR BOX	Six speed
FRAME	Tubular steel spine
WHEELBASE	58.7ins
WEIGHT	474lbs dry
TOP SPEED	136mph

'Invented' by aftermarket specialists, the 900 Sprint quickly became one of the most successful models in the Triumph range, offering a rare brand of performance and practicality.

As well as the rider, the fairing gives the engine an easier time. 100 horsepower shoving a naked Trident through the air has a much tougher time than the same power pushing a comparatively slippery fairing. As with the 900 Daytona, the simple appliance of a dash of aerodynamics makes an already potent engine seem even stronger.

In just a few short years we have come to expect a high standard of finish from Triumph, and the Sprint does not disappoint. The quality of paint and plating is as high as anything in motorcycling, BMW included. Carburation and clutch action are equally refined, and the gear change is superbly precise.

And the three-cylinder engine, of course, is special: flexible, inexhaustible and strong. It thrives on revs, yet punches hard through the mid-range. Like all its siblings, it employs a balance shaft to reduce vibration, but not at the expense of 'character'. Somehow, something distinctive gets through to the rider. You can't quite put your finger on it, but there's a rumble, a cadence, *something*, which says 'I am not a four, and especially not a Japanese four: I am *different*'.

No concealing race-replica styling here, and the Sprint's superb powerplant certainly has no reason to be bashful.

Triumph Thunderbird

....

One glance at the Thunderbird said everything about the bike that Triumph created to spearhead its return to the American market in 1995. The three-cylinder cruiser was built for nostalgia, echoing the British firm's 1950s and '60s look from its high bars and chrome headlamp all the way to its wire wheels and old-style 'peashooter' silencers. The name added to the period feel, too, for the original 650cc Thunderbird parallel twin had been a big US hit for Triumph in the '50s, and was the bike famously ridden by Marlon Brando's character, Johnny, in *The Wild One*.

The Thunderbird represented a big step for the fast-expanding Hinckley firm, as it was the first model to move significantly away from the modular concept on which Triumph's range had been based. Although the basic layout of this bike's watercooled, twin-cam, 12-valve powerplant was shared with the eight other triples in the range, numerous engine and chassis components were unique, making the Thunderbird more complicated and expensive to produce.

Although the T-bird's striking styling slightly compromised its performance, the first Retro Triumph instantly vaulted to the head of Hinckley's sales figures. It now accounts for 30 per cent of total production.

Triumph retained the big triple's familiar 885cc capacity, but the T-bird's cylinder head, crankcases and covers were restyled to mimic those of old aircooled models. Internal changes, including different cams and a lower compression ratio, reduced peak power to 69bhp from the normal 97bhp. Like the Speed Triple, the new triple also had five, rather than Triumph's more common six ratios in its gearbox.

The frame's main spine was similar to the other models', but joined a modified rear section that allowed a slightly lower dual-seat. Bodywork was all new, and did a great job of recapturing the look of the old twins. The classical 'mouth-organ' tank-badge was almost identical to the '50s original. The fuel tank's shape, the chrome carb-covers and wire-spoked wheels (in 18-inch front, 16-inch rear sizes) all added to the period effect.

Triumph's previous triples had been superbly tractable, yet the detuned engine was even stronger at low revs (peak torque arrives at just 4800rpm). Given a handful of throttle, the Triumph surged forwards almost regardless of how far the tacho needle was from its 8500rpm redline. The motor was wonderfully smooth, too, and the gearbox typically slick. Top-end performance was less impressive, as the T-bird began running out of breath well before its modest top speed of 122mph.

The Thunderbird's chassis was well up to containing its engine performance. The frame was stiff, and suspension at both ends firm by cruiser standards. Hard riding, particularly over a series of bumps, sometimes revealed the handling's limitations with a slight twitch. Unlike other Triumphs, this bike made do with a single front disc brake, but it was effective providing the lever was given a solid squeeze.

For short trips and gentle cruising the Thunderbird was comfortable, manoeuvrable and very pleasant indeed. Inevitably, some practicality had been sacrificed to style. This bike's fuel tank held only 3.3 gallons, compared to the 5.5 gallons of most other Triumphs, limiting range to about 100 miles. By then, the wind-blown riding position had normally made the rider glad of a stop, despite the broad and comfortable dual seat.

Triumph offered extra practicality – and style – with a range of accessories including a screen and panniers. But many riders preferred the added retro image of cosmetic options such as traditional two-tone paintwork and rubber knee-pads for the fuel-tank. That carefully cultivated air of nostalgia, combined with good performance and excellent build quality, rapidly made the new Thunderbird a big hit – not just in America but all over the world.

SPECIFICATION: TRIUMPH THUNDERBIRD	
ENGINE	Water-cooled DOHC 12-valve in-line triple
DISPLACEMENT	885cc
HORSEPOWER	69bhp @ 8000rpm
CARBURETTORS	3 x 36mm Mikuni
GEAR BOX	Five speed
FRAME	Tubular steel spine
WHEELBASE	61ins
WEIGHT	484lbs dry
TOP SPEED	122mph

The Thunderbird's name, 'mouth organ' tank badge and acres of chrome plate hark back – and forward? – to an age when Triumph motorcycles ruled America.

Triumph Trophy 1200

The first of revitalised Triumph's modular superbikes caused a sensation when it was released in 1991. A big, four-cylinder machine designed to deliver both performance and comfort, the Trophy 1200 was fast, smooth, stable, sophisticated – a match in almost every department for the very best sports-tourers on the roads. So impressive was the British firm's debut model that it could have been built by one of the Japanese giants.

Instead it had been developed from scratch by the team led by John Bloor, the multi-millionaire builder who had bought bankrupt Triumph from the liquidator in 1983. Bloor then spent eight years secretly building an impressive new factory at Hinckley, not far from Triumph's old Meriden base, and planning a range of modular machines. Three- and four-cylinder engine layouts used alternative crankshafts to produce four different motors. These powered six initial models, the biggest of which was the four-cylinder Trophy.

Apart from its modular construction, which was unique in the bike world, the Trophy's 1180cc engine was conventional. The watercooled in-line four contained 16 valves, worked by twin overhead camshafts, and produced a very respectable maximum of 125bhp at 9000rpm. More impressive still was its crisp carburation and outstanding supply of midrange torque, which made riding the big Triumph delightfully easy and relaxing.

Instant acceleration was available everywhere, from below 2000rpm to the redline at 9500rpm. Simply winding back the throttle sent the Trophy hurtling forward with a breathtaking mixture of power, tractability and smoothness. There were no power steps, just a steady stream of irrepressible torque that sent the Triumph surging towards a top-speed of just over 150mph and made its excellent six-speed gearbox almost redundant. Better still, efficient twin balancer shafts ensured that vibration was minimal at all engine speeds.

Triumph's modular approach was also employed in the chassis, notably the frame, shared

Arguably the most effortless powerplant in motorcycling, the Trophy's is precisely 1¹/₃ Triumph triples. The extra cylinder gives lashings of additional torque to what was already a potent engine.

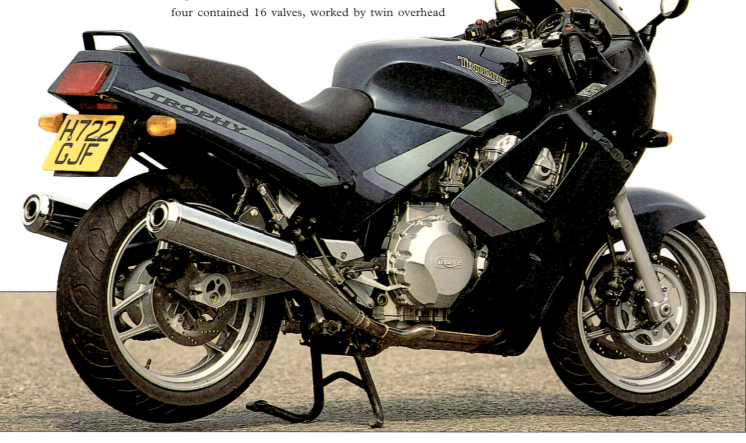

Trophy design has evolved to make it a high-speed mile-eater with few equals . . .

. . . yet it can still do this (left) with startling panache.

by all six models and based around a single large-diameter steel spine that incorporated the engine as a stressed member. The frame held 43mm forks and a vertical rear monoshock, both from Japanese specialists Kayaba. Brakes were also made in Japan, by Nissin. Twin-piston front calipers squeezed a pair of 296mm discs up front, giving braking that was adequate – but no more – in conjunction with the single rear disc.

Although the spine frame design appeared dated in comparison with the latest alloy twin-beam constructions, the Trophy handled very well. In a straight line it was totally stable at all speeds, and barely gave a twitch even in bumpy high-speed curves. Chassis geometry was fairly conservative, and at 529lbs the bike was no lightweight. But the Triumph's steering was neutral, suspension was good and the bike could be hustled along a twisty road at a very respectable rate.

The Trophy's efficient full fairing, large fuel tank and comfortable seat were also well designed. Along with the Triumph's impressive strength and reliability, they combined to create a superb sports-

tourer that was competitive with long-standing Japanese favourites such as Kawasaki's ZZ-R1100 and Yamaha's FJ1200. If the Trophy had a fault, it was simply that its four-cylinder engine layout and conservative styling were unexceptional.

Few riders complained after they'd tried the Trophy 1200, which became a long-standing success for the British firm. In subsequent years it was refined with features including uprated brakes, a lower seat, improved finish and a clock in the dashboard. All helped to make the first new-generation Triumph an even more competent all-round superbike than ever.

'The bike could be hustled along a twisty road at a very respectable rate.'

SPECIFICATION: TRIUMPH TROPHY 1200	
ENGINE	Water-cooled DOHC 16-valve in-line four
DISPLACEMENT	1180cc
HORSEPOWER	125bhp @ 9000rpm
CARBURETTORS	4 x 36mm Mikuni
GEAR BOX	Five speed
FRAME	Tubular steel spine
WHEELBASE	58.7ins
WEIGHT	528lbs dry
TOP SPEED	153mph

Yamaha FJ1200

....

*I*f the expression 'Superbike' sometimes encompasses ephemeral machines which fade as quickly out of the limelight as they flitted in, Yamaha's FJ1200 has proved to be one of the most enduring. A by-word for effortless long-distance work, it is comfortable, practical and fast. Very few bikes demolish miles quite so effortlessly. Until ousted by Triumph's 1200 Trophy (see page 82), it was the yardstick by which four-cylinder grunt was judged. Little wonder, then, that half the motorcycle press seem to have owned a FJ at one time or another.

Like good wine, the big Yamaha has improved progressively with the years. Initially launched in 1984 as the FJ1100, the machine was initially conceived as a sports bike, but soon came to be regarded as the definitive high-speed sports-tourer. In 1986, the engine was bored out from 1097 to 1188cc, adding to the air-cooled engine's already copious mid-range power. In '88 a 17in front wheel belatedly replaced the previous 16 incher, which both helped handling and reduced the front tyre's excessive wear. At the same time the brakes were uprated to four-piston calipers, and hydraulic anti-dive abandoned.

1991 saw the biggest redesign yet. ABS brakes were offered as an option (FJ1200A). A new, sturdier version of the original 'perimeter' frame with rubber-mounted engine replaced the previous chassis, in which the engine was solidly bolted as a stressed member. Throughout its long life the FJ has also received innumerable detail changes, notably to screen and seat, aimed at improving its long-distance capability. At one time a shaft-drive option, as fitted to Yamaha's equally venerable XJ900, was rumoured to be imminent. The 1200, however, steadfastly makes do with a chain.

The heart of the FJ is its engine. Although now dated in concept, it is supremely robust and works superbly on this class of bike – a real autobahn bruiser. Where many other Superbikes rocket to 160mph and well beyond, the FJ12 struggles to reach 150. Several sports 600s are as quick. Yet very few machines are this easy. Bottomless midrange power makes overtaking effortless, and the top gear take-up from 100mph can embarrass more powerful machines. Pre-'91 examples suffer from buzzy vibration at certain revs; later, rubber-mounted models are silky-smooth throughout the range.

With this class of machine, stability and steering are far more important considerations than the ability to flick through chicanes like a Honda Fireblade. The FJ is a big, heavy bike, but carries its weight low. Handling is all-round competent, but marred by somewhat limited ground-clearance two-up. Fitted with the right tyres, it behaves well, but it is very tyre sensitive. Michelin radials seem to work best. The brakes are excellent on later models (the entire front end is the same as the FZR1000's), and the optional ABS anti-lock system is the best on the market.

Add an effective (but not over-large) fairing, a seat more than roomy enough for two, and the ability to lug huge amounts of luggage, and you begin to appreciate the FJ's real-world value. Perhaps its only serious flaw as the ultimate sports tourer is its limited tank range – at 37mpg, you can easily find yourself looking for petrol stations every 150 miles. But despite its age, the big FJ still represents a supremely practical package for the long-haul rider. It is not the quickest Superbike, and it is certainly not the sexiest, but year-in, year-out, it does what many do not: it really works.

'Very few bikes demolish miles quite so effortlessly.'

Compared to more recent superbikes, the FJ's handling is ponderous with a marked lack of ground clearance two-up. Comfort, though, is hard to beat.

SPECIFICATION: YAMAHA FJ1200	
ENGINE	Air-cooled DOHC 16-valve transverse four
DISPLACEMENT	1188cc
HORSEPOWER	125bhp @ 9000rpm
CARBURETTORS	4 x 36mm Mikuni CV
GEAR BOX	Five speed
FRAME	Square-section steel perimeter
WHEELBASE	58.9ins
WEIGHT	546lbs dry
TOP SPEED	146mph

Big air-cooled engine lacks the latest technology, but is a by-word for big-hearted power.

Yamaha FZR1000

Any motorcycle capable of lapping the Isle of Man TT course at over 117mph has got to be special. When the machine in question is a standard roadster, complete with lights, generator and pillion seat, and has since benefited from a further five years of development, it is clearly very special indeed. This is just part of the pedigree of Yamaha's stunning FZR1000.

The big four began life in 1987, immediately capturing the imagination of the motorcycling public and becoming a best-seller. In 1989 it received an extra dose of desirability with the arrival of the EXUP version, then revelled in a further revamp for '94. Throughout it has enjoyed substantially the same 'Genesis' engine technology: a liquid-cooled four with double overhead camshafts and no less than five (three inlet, two exhaust) valves per cylinder.

The advantage of so many valves is two-fold. Since they are small and light, they can therefore tolerate the frantic acceleration and deceleration of ultra-high revs without 'floating' on their springs. Secondly, they offer far more valve area than a two-valve set-up, particularly when partly open, allowing better engine breathing.

Then there is the extra ingredient: EXUP, Yamaha's unique variable exhaust system. This employs a small servo motor to rotate a valve under the engine, which automatically 'tunes' the exhaust system for maximum efficiency at different rpm. The result is the most flexible sports 1000 on the market, a device which both thrives on dizzy revs but hurtles out of turns almost as strongly at mid-range engine speeds. This schizoid character – part full-blown race engine, part tourer – makes the EXUP surpassingly easy to ride quickly.

Full power versions of the EXUP engine offer no less than 147bhp, capable of propelling the FZR to almost 170mph, with shattering quarter mile times comfortably below 11 seconds. For the UK, air 'dams' built into the inlet stubs restrict power to a 'mere' 125bhp. It is likely that this restriction will be abandoned in the near future, but in the meantime the missing horsepower is easily liberated with no more than a sharp knife.

Long gone are the days when Japan built superb engines which utterly outclassed their chassis. Tying the FZR together is a huge aluminium 'Deltabox' frame, stiff as a bridge but infinitely lighter. A huge aluminium swing-arm is similarly rigid. The latest versions of the FZR wear ultra-stiff Öhlins 'upside-down' front forks, and a high specification rear monoshock. Both are adjustable for spring pre-load and damping to suit different riding styles and conditions.

SPECIFICATION:	YAMAHA FZR1000
ENGINE	Liquid-cooled DOHC 20-valve transverse four
DISPLACEMENT	1002cc
HORSEPOWER	125bhp @ 10,000rpm
CARBURETTORS	4 x 37mm Mikuni CV
GEAR BOX	Five speed
FRAME	Aluminium twin beam
WHEELBASE	57.5ins
WEIGHT	471lbs
TOP SPEED	168mph

Centrepiece of the 'EXUP' Yamaha is a huge 'Deltabox' frame of unparalleled stiffness. Other chassis components are similarly sophisticated.

'One finger is all it takes to bring the machine howling down from 150mph to rest.'

Hard-charging FZR is now almost ten years old, but very few mass-produced machines can rival its balance of sheer power and handling.

Although never found wanting in the braking department, 1994 brought a quantum leap with the same six-piston front calipers previously fitted to the YZF750. With six pads biting on two huge 320mm semi-floating rotors, braking power is unsurpassed, sensitivity unparalleled. One finger is all it takes to bring the machine howling down from 150mph to rest with so little drama it is almost disappointing. Along with the new brakes and forks came a re-style which makes the FZR look 20mph faster than before, even sitting still.

This combination of fierce but controllable power, top-quality running gear and impeccable stability and steering make the FZR1000 not only one of the fastest point-to-point bikes in creation, but a beguilingly easy beast to ride quickly. Less frantic and raw than Suzuki's GSX-R1100, more agile than Kawasaki's ZZ-R, only Honda's much newer Fireblade runs it close. The FZR1000 is simply one of the all-time great motorcycling experiences.

Yamaha GTS1000

··························

When it comes to bringing technological innovation to mass-produced motorcycles, Yamaha leads the way with its revolutionary GTS1000.

The GTS was the first mass-production superbike of the modern age to use a front suspension system that didn't employ a pair of telescopic forks and a chassis that doesn't run more or less in a straight line from the steering head to the swingarm pivot.

Motorcycle manufacturers have long searched for a method of suspending the front wheel of a motorcycle that doesn't rely on conventional telescopic forks. 'Teles' are unsatisfactory for several reasons – they are prone to flexing under braking and when cornering, and then cause the front end of the bike to 'dive' under braking. The search for a realistic alternative has been the Holy Grail of motorcycle engineering.

Yamaha's alternative front end, as featured on the GTS1000, is a single-sided front swingarm with hub-centre steering not unlike one front wheel of a car. Separating the steering function from the

suspension should, in theory, produce a bike that steers, corners and brakes better than a bike with conventional forks.

The GTS's Omega chassis is different from that of a conventional bike because the front suspension removes the necessity for a headstock. The aluminium-alloy frame is a squat box-shaped affair which wraps around the engine, on to which are bolted the front and rear suspension systems, as well as the sub-frames necessary for the steering, seat and bodywork.

So how does this alternative front suspension system work? Basically it's in two parts. A single-sided swingarm attaches the front wheel to the chassis and a single shock-absorber bolts between the two. The steering is handled separately by a vertical cast aluminium-alloy spar that goes from the front axle to a steering box and thence to the handlebar crown.

The result is a bike that has one of the most sophisticated front suspension systems in production. The bad news is that, in the case of the GTS at least, this kind of suspension system offers no significant improvement over conventional telescopic forks. Being designed as a sports-touring

Bold styling and high price of Yamaha's 'flagship' GTS has tempered sales, but expect to see more such technology on future models.

motorcycle the GTS is too long and carries too much weight to reap any benefits from hub-centre steering other than the elimination of front end dive under braking.

Indeed, the GTS is actually slower steering and more ponderous than many of its competitors, which surely isn't what Yamaha intended. Oddly enough, the harder the GTS is ridden the better it responds, which gives credence to claims that this is the way forward for sports bikes. It just doesn't seem to suit 550lb sports-tourers too well.

But what of the rest of the GTS? The engine is a state-of-the-art, 100bhp fuel-injected 1000cc in-line four with five valves per cylinder. The exhaust system features a three-way catalytic converter, and a tamper-proof ignition system. The front brake is also worthy of mention. The single-sided front swingarm means that only one disc brake can be fitted to the GTS, so Yamaha have equipped the GTS's single 320mm ventilated disc with a six-piston caliper for stupendous stopping power.

The GTS's performance is brisk rather than

exceptional, with a top-speed nudging 140mph. Although it shares the same basic layout as the Yamaha FZR1000, modifications to the valve timing and the fuel-injection system, ensure that the GTS only puts out 100bhp but with a substantial increase in mid-range power.

The GTS1000 is technologically very ambitious, and presents some interesting solutions to age-old problems. But ultimately it is an example of technology for technology's sake rather than a major step forward in motorcycle design.

Sure-footedness of the GTS's novel front suspension comes into its own on bumpy Lakeland back roads such as these.

SPECIFICATION: YAMAHA GTS1000	
ENGINE	Liquid-cooled DOHC 20-valve in-line four
DISPLACEMENT	1002cc
HORSEPOWER	100bhp @ 9000rpm
CARBURETTORS	Electronic fuel injection
GEAR BOX	Five speed
FRAME	Aluminium-alloy Omega twin beam
WHEELBASE	58.8ins
WEIGHT	542lbs dry
TOP SPEED	140mph

'The result is a bike that has one of the most sophisticated front suspension systems in production.'

Yamaha V-Max 1200

'Trying to go fast on a V-Max anywhere other than a straight line is not a relaxing experience!'

It's too big, too fat, too heavy, it won't stop and it doesn't handle. But – my! – is it *fast*.

By the mid-'eighties, motorcycle design had come a long way. From the early, over-powered and ill-handling Japanese superbikes, had evolved machines which took their cues from the racetrack and had tyres, suspension and steering to match. Suzuki's GSX-R750 and Yamaha's FZ750 typified the new breed.

But there will always be those who are less concerned with all-round performance than with sheer, brute power and the thrill of violent standing start acceleration. The Yamaha V-Max was designed just for them.

When it was first introduced in 1985, the V-Max caused a sensation, as much for its styling as its potential performance. The high-barred, low-slung look was based on the American cruiser style – bikes made for showing off in illegal sprints on impromptu drag strips on public roads. Real drag

bikes had already evolved into long-wheelbased, front-heavy machines designed specifically for speed. Cruiser style puts the emphasis on *looking* fast – lots of noise and the ability to leave long strips of burnt rubber off the startline are more important than actual times.

And with a claimed 145bhp, the V-Max was capable of leaving a line of rubber all the way to the horizon – rear tyres on V-Maxes live short and tortured, but exciting lives.

The V-Max is completely dominated by its engine. At the time its V-four layout was a high-tech departure from the in-line fours that powered most Japanese motorcycles (only Honda built V-fours in any numbers). It featured a novel carburettor arrangement which meant each cyclinder was fed by two carburettors, then a gate moved to allow those same two carburettors to fill a different cylinder, thus eliminating the 'dead' time that usually occurs during a bike's combustion cycle. The result was midrange power that was literally like nothing any rider had experienced before, without sacrificing peak power. For a four cylinder engine it made its power at comparatively low revs – the red line was at just 8,500rpm. Visually, the massive black and silver V-four is the centrepiece of the bike's styling. And once on the move, the slightly lumpy power delivery – and the sheer amount of power it delivers – distract attention from the bike's handling.

It was the handling, more than the excess of power, that got the V-Max a reputation as a bike for would-be He-Men. It weaves, it wobbles, and it has so little ground clearance that a cornering V-Max strikes showers of sparks wherever it goes. The tyres are built for long life, not grip, and the brakes are only just about up to the job of hauling the V-Max's bulk down from speed. Trying to go fast on a V-Max anywhere other than a straight line is not a relaxing experience!

None of this matters to V-Max owners. Most don't even care that the top speed is 'only' 140mph. For a start, the lack of a fairing means hanging on at anything over 100mph is gruelling work. No, V-Max owners know that for that moment when the lights change to green (whether on the drag strip or the high street) what matters is how quickly and impressively the bike gets off the line.

In this, the V-Max is the motorcycling equivalent of the huge American muscle cars of the 'seventies – built for fun in a land where the speed limit is 55mph. It may not be the fastest or best-handling bike available, but it's become a modern classic for one reason – there is nothing else in Creation quite like a V-Max.

SPECIFICATION: YAMAHA V-MAX	
ENGINE	Water-cooled DOHC 16-valve V-four
DISPLACEMENT	1198cc
HORSEPOWER	145bhp @ 8000rpm
CARBURETTORS	4 x 35mm Mikuni
GEAR BOX	Five speed
FRAME	Steel cradle
WHEELBASE	62.6ins
WEIGHT	578lbs dry
TOP SPEED	140mph

Whether it's a standard V-Max (right) or a special such as the Egli (below), only the devastating punch of the imposing V-four engine really matters. UK versions, sadly, have their power restricted.

Yamaha XJR1200

....

*'Acceleration
was fearsome
above
4000rpm.'*

When Yamaha decided to enter the retro-bike market with a big, unfaired four-cylinder roadster, the perfect powerplant was already close to hand. The FJ1200 sports-tourer had been hugely popular for years due largely to its superbly tractable air cooled, 16-valve engine. This faithful brute of a motor was detuned, its cylinder fin-tips were polished, and it was put on display at the heart of a twin-shock musclebike called the XJR1200.

Yamaha lacked the four-stroke tradition of Kawasaki and Honda, whose Zephyr and CB1000 models the XJR was created to challenge. But the new bike's lines contained a hint of the 1978-model XS1100 four, and its all-black colour scheme echoed that of the later XS1100S Midnight Special. Maybe the lack of an illustrious predecessor was an advantage, because the clean, simply styled XJR was an undeniably good-looking machine.

The 1188cc motor was placed in a new round-tube steel frame which, like the square-section FJ frame, incorporated a bolt-on lower rail to allow engine removal. Forks were conventional 43mm units, while at the back the XJR had a pair of remote-reservoir shocks from Öhlins, the Swedish suspension specialist firm owned by Yamaha. A pair of broad 17-inch wheels, the front holding big 320mm front discs with four-piston calipers, completed a purposeful profile.

From the rider's conveniently low seat the Yamaha gave a view of slightly raised handlebars, and chrome-rimmed instruments with a central fuel gauge. The engine contained numerous internal modifications to bring peak power output down to 97bhp at 8000rpm, from the FJ1200's 123bhp, and developed even more of the addictive low-rev torque for which the big four had long been renowned. Not that the motor hinted at the power waiting within, as it fired up with a mechanical rustle and a restrained burble from short twin silencers.

The upright riding position and that big, lazy engine set the tone of the bike, encouraging gentle riding and minimal use of the smooth-shifting five-speed gearbox. The XJR responded crisply from as

FJ1200-based engine is the ideal candidate for a Retro musclebike. In XJR form, the air-cooled four puts out even more mid-range torque.

low as 2000rpm in top gear, which made for effortless overtaking, and remained impressively smooth at almost all engine speeds. Acceleration was fearsome above 4000rpm, the handlebars tugging hard at the rider's shoulders as the Yamaha surged smoothly forward. If you hung on and kept the throttle open, it kept pulling remorselessly all the way to 140mph.

Handling was competent for this class of machine and the XJR remained stable at speed, despite the forces being fed into it by the human parachute at the handlebars. The Yamaha always felt like a fairly big, heavy bike, but it changed direction without a great deal of effort. Suspension at both ends was compliant enough for a comfortable ride, but firm enough to allow reasonably spirited cornering. Dunlop's fat radial tyres gave more than enough grip to exploit all the available ground-clearance, and the big front disc brakes were superbly powerful.

Japanese riders were the first to discover this first-hand, as the XJR was introduced as a home-market bike in 1994, before being released elsewhere a year later. Most of those who rode it were impressed. Inevitably, the XJR1200 shared the limitations of every big naked bike, in that the exposed riding position soon made using the engine's top-end performance tiring. But the big four's flexible power delivery made up for that. And the Yamaha's solid handling, handsome looks and general feel of quality made the XJR many riders' choice as the best big retro-bike of all.

SPECIFICATION: YAMAHA XJR1200	
ENGINE	Air-cooled DOHC 16-valve in-line four
DISPLACEMENT	1188cc
HORSEPOWER	97bhp @ 8000rpm
CARBURETTORS	4 x 37mm Mikuni
GEAR BOX	Five speed
FRAME	Tubular steel
WHEELBASE	58.5ins
WEIGHT	488lbs dry
TOP SPEED	140mph

Yamaha were late to clamber on board the Retro bandwagon, but the brutally handsome XJR1200 hits the spot.

Wide 'bars and upright riding position make the big Yamaha surprisingly agile through the turns, but this is still a massive machine to throw around.

Yamaha YZF750

Yamaha's FZ750 had been one of the company's best-sellers in the mid-'eighties, but by the early 'nineties it was dated – outhandled and outpowered by a new generation of alloy-framed, fat-tyred race replicas. Rumours of a replacement had been rife since Kawasaki launched the ZXR750 in 1989. But at that time Yamaha's answer was to launch the OW01, (a limited edition – and extremely expensive – World Superbike contender), and let the FZ soldier on as a road bike.

But by late 1992, the OW01 had also reached the end of its potential in world-class competition – now it was time to build a bike for the racetrack as well as the road.

The YZF750 was launched at the beginning of 1993 and quickly got a name for itself as a nimble, quick-steering sportster that handled more like a 600 than a big 750. It was based on the well-proven OW01 design, but developed to the point where no parts are interchangeable between the two.

Importantly for road riders, the YZF's road manners didn't need to be compromised by its track aspirations. A limited-edition SP version was built for racing, with a close-ratio gearbox, stiffer, multi-adjustable suspension, a single race seat and huge carburettors. That left the standard YZF with more useable gear ratios, proper pillion accommodation and far better engine behaviour than the SP. In fact, only the SP's adjustable suspension made YZF owners jealous. Yamaha listened to them and the standard YZF soon sprouted fully-adjustable Öhlins suspension front and rear.

The new suspension helped to make an already quick-steering and sweet-handling bike into a real road weapon. Surprisingly for a 750, it's easy to handle on twisty backroads, and civilised enough to cover long distances in reasonable comfort. That's partly down to the quality of the suspension, which allows relatively soft springs without compromising control – bumpy bends don't throw the YZF off line, or throw the rider out of his seat. But if you really want to experience the YZF's mind-expanding limits safely you need smooth, open roads or the freedom of a race track.

Because the YZF is fast. Not just in terms of outright speed – Kawasaki's ZXR is a little faster in still conditions. What makes the YZF's engine

Better looking and far, far cheaper than the Yamaha OW01 from which it is derived, the YZF is the classiest transverse four in the 750cc division.

Despite its superb credentials as a road bike, the YZF has never quite had the development to deliver in world superbike competition. The potential, though, is certainly there.

'The new suspension helped to make an already quick-steering and sweet-handling bike into a real road weapon.'

special is its smooth, linear midrange power delivery. For this, we have to thank Yamaha's unique EXUP system. The EXUP (it stands for Exhaust Ultimate Powervalve) is a valve in the exhaust collector pipe that opens and closes at pre-set revs, and fools the engine into thinking it has an exhaust pipe specifically tuned for those revs. The result is apparent as soon as you ride the YZF – where its competitors have little low-down pull, followed by peak power coming in with a bang, the YZF just pulls, and pulls, and pulls, from 3,000rpm all the way to the 13,000rpm redline.

Slowing the YZF down from its 160mph+ top speed are some of the most powerful front brakes fitted to any road bike. Twin discs are gripped so hard by six-piston calipers it's not unknown for the discs to warp under the strain. Other bikes now wear six-piston brakes (including some Triumphs and Suzukis), but the YZF was the first production bike to boast them as standard.

But its instant success as a road bike wasn't to be mirrored on the track. It was to be late 1994 before the YZF proved its worth and achieved its first serious international success – victory at the Bol d'Or 24-hour race in the hands of brothers and ex-GP racers Christian and Dominique Sarron. The race bike had finally caught up with the road bike.

SPECIFICATION: YAMAHA YZF750	
ENGINE	Water-cooled DOHC 20-valve in-line four
DISPLACEMENT	749cc
HORSEPOWER	122bhp @ 12,000rpm
CARBURETTORS	4 x 38mm Mikuni
GEAR BOX	Six speed
FRAME	Deltabox aluminium twin beam
WHEELBASE	55.9ins
WEIGHT	432lbs
TOP SPEED	160mph

YZF's 'Fox-eye' headlamps and superb six-piston front brakes set a trend. Its performance simply sets the pulse racing.

Index

···